Praise for *Break Through - The Wisdom of the Soul*

"The chapter *Go Ahead and Kill Me* is intriguing and refreshingly unrepentant. The writing is revealing and riveting. I felt every word! I received new found gratitude and strength to overcome my own struggles. Looking forward to more from the author Siobhan Morse!"

-Rebecca Jiampetti

"Sue Lapp's story *This One Vessel* touched on my life as a child. Her courage to share her story of alcoholism and bad choices for 30 years will enlighten many in how easy it is to fall into the hell of addiction.

I love this story as it shows just how a long, tough journey can sometimes bring you right back to where you were supposed to be all along."

- Dora Sherry, author of *Reflections of an Angel - A Journey of Loss, Abuse and Recovery from Opioid Addiction*

"Oh, what a delight *Quacking Up*, by Felicia Brown proved to be. Brown details the story of how she used a simple little rubber duck as her one thing that made her smile, that brought the tiniest bit of joy back to a world gone mad. Bravo on a job well done and for making this reader smile."

- Lynn Chandler Willis, Award-winning and best-selling author of Shamus Award finalist, *Wink of an Eye*, and the *Ava Logan Mystery Series*.

"POWERFUL, INSIGHTFUL, REFLECTIVE, STIRRING INTROSPECTION. A mesmerizing insight into a powerful personal journey, from an unspeakable murky abyss, into the light of a new dawn by Author Theresa Neale as she eloquently recounts and chronicles the effects of an early path of unspeakable darkness, to mastering its pitfalls to become a presence of profound and brilliant illumination."

- Sheila Clark, Medium, Teacher and Healer

"I was immediately drawn to this book. Amy's heartfelt words as a mother and as an advocate for her son resonated with me as I have experienced similar highs and lows with my own son's journey. The struggles, the joys, the triumphs, and the reminder that love conquers all encourages me and reminds me that my son and I are not alone and that others have walked the same two-spirited path. This book is warm, engaging and refreshingly real. I highly recommend it!"

– *Deborah Myers*, Paralegal and LGBTQIA Ally

"Reading this story brought back to life many of my own traumas and issues surrounding the crushing of the soul religion can bring. It is wonderful to read this poignant story and be reminded there is a path to true love of self, peace and happiness."

-*Shane Lewis*

"Such an inspiring read! Daphne takes us along her journey from her unorthodox childhood to her desire to raise her own children in a similar fashion. We get to know her through heartbreak, comedy of errors, awakening and eventually triumph! It's such an inspiring story because it's so encouraging with it's "small positive changes add up" approach. A real joy to read."

– *Nicole Watson*

BREAK THROUGH

WISDOM OF THE SOUL

Powerful Potential and Purpose Publishing

First printing, October 2020

Cover art, graphics and book design by Candy Lyn Thomen - www.CandyLynCreates.com

ISBN: 978-1-7349655-5-1

Published in USA

www.PPP-Publishing.com
Hickory, NC - USA

DEDICATION

To our souls – you have sprinkled wisdom upon the cells of our life so we re-member our purpose.

To the souls who contributed with fearless vulnerability as they have awakened to levels of new insight that may help one person who is guided to receive

To our creator, you infuse us with divine secrets so that our gardens will grow and our hearts will open.
Thank you for the universal wisdom that awaits each of us.

To Christan —

Remember "Fair" is something you go to in the summertime. It's got nothing to do with life

Love
Sue

Break Through - Wisdom of the Soul

Contents

Break Through - The Wisdom of the Soul

Introduction

A cry from the soul, could that be your spiritual awakening?

When we begin to doubt our life, career, world events, indoctrinations religious or otherwise, there is an inner sense and knowing, 'waking us up' to breakthrough and transform our lives.

I know for myself when my brother died at thirty-nine unexpectedly, it woke me up to my personal relationship challenges, and other things I was internally struggling with in my life. I knew there was something more, and the timely passing of my sibling showed me how precious every moment in life is, and how we spend it.

Whatever the reason, your soul wisdom is already undergoing something right now, whether or not you are consciously aware of it. The tragedies, loss, health crises and other milestones in life will trigger something within us to look at things differently. The unsettling feelings or emptiness we experience is an initiation to the gateway of insight, if we choose.

Have you noticed, perhaps, you cannot really plan for them, even when you think you have control over your path, something will show up to teach you more than you imagined? Perhaps a hidden gift emerges, or a profound realization more fulfilling shows up in your life. You realize the external world was not bringing this longing to its deepest fulfillment possible. The illusions may even depress you or create anxiety, as you attempt to figure things out. This can feel nearly impossible, because you are not necessarily equipped on a conscious level to know your potential. However, eventually it will shake you up.

Have you questioned your purpose in life? Do you wonder why you are really here? Has it occurred to you that life's challenges, obstacles and tragedies are part of your awakening and can be the most significant time to examine your fundamental core beliefs?

Our authors have questioned everything from their religious beliefs about God and a higher state of consciousness, to sensing deep losses physically and emotionally in their lives. You can feel their Dark Night of the Soul journey in several of the stories, harrowing experiences which shook them to their core, and perhaps had to experience unimaginable pain. I can relate to many life events, where some higher wisdom, God, unconscious, whatever you desire to call it, would hit me over my head to 'wake me up'.

How do you know you are having a spiritual awakening and it's not a typical life event most people seem to have? We all go through it, not all of us choose to wake up through it. The doubt, the questioning, the fear and even loneliness can stop us from pursuing further. We may think chronic health issues are merely part of the aging process, when a part of you is actually dying, because your life force energy is dwindling.

Our spiritual wisdom wants to show us our purpose. It is a natural way of the soul evolving and expanding as we mature. Just like a flower grows and blooms, so does our connection with our soul. It becomes a conscious effort at significant periods of transformation to learn more about the fulfillment and peace waiting for us. Some wait for their death beds to explore this, while others will come into the world with a knowing to pursue it at an early age; although not fully understanding the process, because we didn't have an instruction booklet upon our birth. You will learn how each author is at different stages of their awakening, you may relate to several or one in particular. It is the hope of each of us, to help you find a more meaningful life, freedom and self-love.

We ask that you do not feel sorry for the journey, the awakening process because it was through this pain, disturbing at first, which gave each one a more meaningful life. There will be unique moments and times in our life when we can go deeper into our spiritual path and awaken to another level of higher consciousness, wisdom and purpose.

Yes, your soul will tug on you, and the more you become aware how disconnected you may be from your divine connection, your God source, you will realize how profoundly entwined this process is physically, mentally, emotionally and spiritually. Eventually your perspective will shift, no longer seeing your life as you did in your previous state of complacent awareness. At the time of writing and publishing this book in 2020, a massive awakening of truth and consciousness shift was happening. Many walked this dark night of the soul, questioning everything, wondering what is true? It was a great time of transpersonal exploration, and to integrate conscious habits that will profoundly have one experiencing a tremendous shift, accessing levels of new wisdom for their life journey. A mystical experience may have united you with your soul essence. While full self-realization is a process, you, non-the-less, can feel a new connection which helps you obtain 'spiritual peace', eliminating the fear of the chaos and confusion that still exists in one's life or the world at large.

If you feel like your life or what you have been taught is 'false', you will question more. You may notice there is no joy in what you used to do, because the veil of illusion is falling away. The craving becomes stronger with each step you take to access your soul wisdom, even if you are still unsure what that may be for you. It is not uncommon to purge people and things from your life. You may come to realize you no longer want 'possessions', and you may stumble upon something new one day that opens a whole unknown world for you, what seemingly feels by accident.

The intention of Breakthrough and all these stories is to provide a sense of insight for the various stages and different ways one may experience the portal, the gateway opening to their inner wisdom. As we continue to explore, our intuition will heighten. You may desire to contribute to the world in another way. You may help others and you may just realize for the first time you really are whole and complete now that you found self-love.

Enjoy the journey, embrace the detours while trusting the process.

~ *Gloria Coppola*, Best-Selling Author, Spiritual Minister and Publisher

"The dark night of the soul is a journey into light, a journey from your darkness into the strength and hidden resources of your soul."

– Carolyn Myss

Daphne is a registered nurse, Kundalini yoga instructor, Reiki Master, certified Dr. Sears health coach, intuitive reader, and former homebirth midwife of nine years.

She is an avid traveler, loves good food, a life-long learner, blogger, wife, mother of five (one in heaven), enjoys helping others find their truth, their *Sat Nam* and beckoning harmony into this world of unknowns.

https://beckoningharmony.com/

IG: @beckoning_harmony

Offering Reiki, Health Coaching, Cacao Ceremonies, and Intuitive Readings

Daphne
Weinheimer McIntosh

Registered Nurse, Reiki Master,
Certified Dr. Sears Health Coach, Intuitive Reader

*"I hope you see things
that startle you.*

*I hope you feel things you
never felt before.*

*I hope you meet people with
a different point of view.*

*I hope you live a life
you're proud of.*

*If you find that you're not,
I hope you have the strength
to start all over again."*

– Eric Roth

Beckoning Harmony

Growing up in a messy and loud family with five girls and two boys, you can only imagine the fun times we had. Instead of fancy vacations, we would go camping or boating at the lake. I never knew any differently. It was a blast.

Most people thought we were an unusual family, although I didn't understand why. We were raised in a religious and conservative home. I was home schooled most of my life. I enjoyed being home schooled, as I could read, bake to my heart's content, and sew. These were the things I most enjoyed, aside from being outside and the camping trips we took! I was so glad I was able to experience learning in this way, as it helped me be open to the possibility of home schooling my own kids one day.

Perhaps children today can't relate to growing up without a T.V. and only allowed to listen to classical, opera or Christian music, like I did. It was a normal life to me. I would though, sometimes, listen to "secular" music if I hung out with my cousins. Shh, don't tell!

As a child, I read a lot about angels and other miracles in the Bible, so I was open to the possibility of actually seeing them. Yes, I was the kid who actually saw angels. I even had one rescue me. I was driving down a country dirt road, after a math tutoring session, when I slid into a small ditch. I started to panic, then thought to pray for help. I didn't have a cell phone back then and houses were far and few between. As soon as I opened my eyes, coming up behind me I saw a red truck. Out stepped a glorious looking man, with long golden hair. I gasped; this was the same angel I had seen other times when I had prayed for help! He didn't say a word. Smiling, he hooked a chain to the minivan, and pulled me right out. The next instant, he was gone! Just like that.

My Dad grew up in Brazil. When I was three, we

were fortunate enough to experience his culture by moving there temporarily. While I don't recall a ton about those times. I do remember how happy the people seemed and all the delicious fruit. The fruit was amazing and there were banana trees lining the streets! One of my favorite foods from Brazil is called Pao de Queijo, a delicious cheese roll made from cassava root flour. I would get to travel to Brazil many times throughout my childhood, teaching me the joy of traveling later in life.

These were highlights of my childhood, getting to experience the warmth of the friendly Brazilians and their fun-loving culture filled with music, food, and beaches. Growing up in many regions of the world, made life very fortunate for me. Such as, Montana, where I would live on an Indian reservation. Imagine what it was like attending pow-wows, wearing moccasins, and braiding our own hair into braids to match theirs. Louisiana was another state I lived in. I believe this may be how I began to appreciate the variety of authentic foods and different cultures.

The local Cajun accent was fun, tasty creole food with spicy crawfish and delectable French pastries.

The way I was raised helped shape me to who I am today. I don't care to live by today's standards. I break through the conventions of society to live in a way that makes sense to me and is the most fulfilling.

We tried for a while to fit into the norm of society. Big houses, fancy cars and motorboats were bought without a thought. This, though, was after the death of my third daughter, which was traumatic for both my husband and I. 30 weeks of pregnancy flew by while being busy with two toddlers. It was then my belly started growing exponentially. After testing, the OB thought my unborn daughter had an issue with her esophagus, which could be fixed immediately after birth. Originally, a homebirth was planned. Now the pregnancy was considered high risk. At only 33 weeks along, I went into labor. It was so sudden and so early. When she was born, they placed her on my chest, but she wasn't soft and squishy like my other babies. The medical staff whisked her away and I felt such a loss. A loss of control and a sense that maybe I had somehow caused this? No, it was nothing I had done, and she had a rare disorder where her cerebellum didn't form. She wouldn't be able to survive without this vital part of the brain. I was devastated. To lose a child so suddenly and unexpectedly is surreal.

The next two years went by in a blur, being on call 24/7 and running my own midwifery business.

During this time, with no room in this crazy busy life, I was losing a sense of self, of my dreams of a happy family. It was in 2014 when my fourth child was born, and I was overwhelmed. How would I be able to keep my on-call job and take care of a new infant? This was a blessing in my life, and I wanted to be there for her. As I explored what this meant to me, I delved deeply into the life I wanted.

I started to read about minimalism. I craved a simpler life. It sounded wonderful. This might be what could get us there. I found out about child-directed learning during this time and thought it would work well for one of my children, who struggled with traditional teaching methods.

In my search, I stumbled across a group of families on Facebook who traveled full-time in an RV. Immediately I became intrigued. My mind started to turn this over. Could this be an answer to my need for harmony in my life? Would I be able to travel with my husband? He had a job where he travelled 95% of the time. When I mentioned the idea about living in a RV, traveling full-time, and simplifying our life to him, it was met with resistance. He wasn't too keen on giving up his nice home and be thrown into a 400 square foot thing on wheels!

I continued my research and joined the online groups of families who travelled full-time in an RV. I saw the fun, connection, and simplicity of their lives on the road. I kept talking about it to my husband. After bringing it up for almost a year, my husband decided to go for it. He was interested in being able to spend more time with me and the kids. He also saw how stressed and frazzled I was being home all week alone, while he was on a travel assignment.

Next, I set out to purge my stuff. Even though our home looked sparse, it was 4,500 square feet and goodness, there was so much stuff hiding about! I pulled out the necessities needed for this type of living, room by room. I read the comments from the online groups I was in to see what I would actually need. We had garage sales, donated, and gave away just about everything, except for select paintings, photos, and some nicer furniture. These we put in a small storage unit on my parent's property.

Finally, the day came to move into our RV. I was excited, but also nervous. What if my family hated living in a RV? Did I make the right choice? We chose a motorhome with bunk beds for the three girls. Our RV had everything one would need for the comforts of life. A full-sized refrigerator, convection oven/microwave, two bathrooms, T.V.s.

Also, the best thing for parents with little kids, blackout curtains for nighttime, when traveling to a different time zone! It took all day to get the RV packed and organized. My kids enjoyed setting up their own bunk areas and sticking photos of friends and family on the wall of their bunk beds.

Imagine my surprise, living my dream, getting to travel full time, only to find out my husband now gets a call he was approved for back surgery! Sure, I should be happy for him. It's great news, right? His pain had gone on for so long. Nothing was easing it. Why now? All our plans, our new adventure, was going to be put on hold. The harmony I beckoned for in my prayers was delayed, yet again.

Our good friends rescued us and graciously allowed us to park our huge RV on their property while he recovered from surgery.

I was about to learn many things over the next six weeks and gosh, is it a funny story!

Little setbacks were happening almost daily. I was so eager to get back on the road. However, the physician said my husband should not be driving yet, even though the surgery was successful. These setbacks came with feelings, nudges, inner intuition, and my own internal guidance system, helping me become flexible. I obviously needed to learn something I wasn't aware of yet or had been neglecting.

The first time I went to drain the gray tank (this is the tank which holds the water residue from sinks, showers, and washing machine), I didn't know to check if the valves were shut, before unscrewing the cap to put the hose attachment on it. A major newbie fail occurred! In all my years of being a mother, midwife, nanny, and nurse, I've never been covered in such disgusting substance covering me from head to toe! The valve from the black tank (the tank holding the residue from toilets) wasn't shut. I learned the hard way on this one! It has been a funny story to tell on the road over the years!

For those six weeks, my daughters had fun learning about farming and selling at farmers markets, as our friend's son was a farmer. They enjoyed pulling beets and loading watermelon into the bed of the truck. It was fun gathering eggs and selling them on the vegetable stand by the road. It was a great time for them. We were able to apply some de-schooling.

I had always wanted to home school my children. Now I had the chance. What I had discovered, when searching for different styles of teaching and learning, was in many circumstances, children needed time to adjust from traditional school to a home school setting. A book I found helpful was one called, *Free To Live: Create a Thriving Unschooling Home* by Pam Laricchia. This is where I had learned about de-schooling, which is taking time from structured learning, while the child adjusts to a non-traditional based learning style. Another book I found helpful was, *Homegrown*, by Ben Hewitt. This style of schooling really called to me. Unschooling allows a child to focus on what they enjoy learning and doing. Though my husband wasn't sure of this style and asked if our daughters could incorporate some basic learning into their day. I then found a book by Purva Brown called, *The Classical Unschooler: Education Without School.* This sounded exactly what my family needed for a balanced school day. I loved seeing my children excited about learning and I enjoyed learning with them too! To be involved in their day to day activities was quite an experience. I was seeing more of what brought them joy during these six weeks than I had in a while. I also was getting to spend more time with my husband, since he was off on medical leave from work. This time was a much-needed break for us from our normal pace of life just a month ago, living in a sticks and bricks home (what full time RV'ers call houses).

Our first trip out of our home state wasn't exactly what I thought it would be like. My husband didn't either because we weren't on the same wavelength about this new lifestyle. He thought paying for a park was a bit pricey.

My parents suggested we put in full hook-ups for our RV on their property. While being with my parents and living small was great, I itched for travel and adventure. I had always been a travel bug (Brazil!) and loved exploring new places. Plus, why did we get an RV anyway if not to travel? My husband and children were comfortable, I was not. My soul ached to be free from "normal" life.

While sitting still, I was able to listen to my intuition, which was nudging me to reach out and get some encouragement from fellow RV'ers. I found a family coach on one of my full-time RV online forums who was highly recommended. She and her family travelled full time in an RV. I felt I could relate to her and hoped my husband would be able to get more insight into how another family managed costs while on the road. She did help us: setting up a budget, finding a membership for RV parks where we would get great discounts, and come to an agreement to travel. A big bonus, she showed us how to do it more leisurely to help acclimate the family to this new lifestyle. Now, we all felt better prepared to do this! Off we went to our new adventure of exploring the United States. With the RV park membership, it provided us with an amazing group of friends, who were part of the membership too. It was fun to connect with them along our travels. These folks were families, just like ours, who craved a simpler life and who had a taste for adventure.

Being a full time RV family has been such fun! We have met some amazing people and have seen awesome parts of our country. My children have had a blast meeting so many new friends along the way. They loved exploring each new area we stopped at. My husband enjoys talking to new acquaintances at each RV park. While it has been the typically ups and downs of life in general, this lifestyle of living small and being in close contact with each family member, we have learned to adjust and grow closer to each other. We got to try out different types of native foods in each state we visited. All of us learned more about the history of the U.S. than any history textbook written. We learned what is most important to ourselves and the family. We know experiencing something together as a family is a lasting memory, whereas most stuff we purchase is forgotten or thrown out. To be closer as a family, knowing time goes so quickly with those we love. Making our family our priority over riches of the world. My family are my jewels. Ones I will treasure throughout eternity.

Society has encouraged us for too long to conform a certain way, obtain a certain look, get a certain job, require a certain type of degree. It doesn't have to be so. I am not bound to the world's view. I create my own life; however the universe may turn me or throw a curve ball at me. YOU are capable of this. Ask yourself, what is it you want more than anything else in this life of yours? Don't wait any longer, now is the time to go for it. If you fall, you will get back up and survive. Gravity holds us on this earth, but we are souls that can fly higher than we ever thought possible. The sky is not the limit. If you feel you don't have what it takes to make a leap such as I did, no worries, just start small. Every step will get you there no matter if they're small ones. I finally feel freed up from "normal" life! It was a time to reconnect with my family and husband. Our life became more harmonious when we chose to leave consumerism and enjoy minimalism. This way of living is very different. I have found many more people now embrace this lifestyle, living their dreams, living for their truth. The freedom I felt wasn't just from being able to travel. It was I had freed my heart and was living my truth, my Sat Nam. Sat Nam is a mantra from Kundalini Yoga. I was awakened from my spiritual slump and my mind expanded beyond my expectations when I started practicing Kundalini Yoga. I am now a certified instructor. Even though I had an enlightened childhood, I found myself stuck in the formality of what I should be. Embracing the unknown with my family of five was so much more than I was ever taught. It is what beckoned harmony into my life. Beckoning harmony is a series of events leading up to this point in my life. I didn't see it at the time. Do we ever? This harmony and my truth was always there, in me. I didn't see myself for my full worth or know my truth, my authentic self. For so long, I had been beckoned by society's standards, not my own.

Traveling, like we do, has opened up the opportunity to talk about why we went on this journey into minimalism, small living, full time travel, unschooling, and family-oriented daily living. It has blessed me with more time to focus on family and relationships. In downsizing our living space, it freed up more time to spend doing what I enjoy than spending hours knee deep in housekeeping and laundry. Minimalistic ideas helped to create a home environment free of clutter and we learned we didn't need so much clothes or stuff. We do follow one set rule: one thing in, one thing out, no matter what.

I look back not in regret or anger, but in love and light that I was so divinely held and gently nudged along the bumps in my life. When I tuned all the noise of the world out and listened to what my authentic self-wanted, I felt at peace. I want others to feel this same way.

The change was not about traveling and the scenery changing, it was that I felt released from expectations I had made for myself. Me being in perfect control. Traveling full-time, in an RV with five kids, a husband and a dog, made me realize I definitely wasn't in control!

Not everyone has to experience tragedy in their lives to find balance. Change up the way you've been thinking about life. Be open to possibilities. Be open to reach out to others for help as I did. Times are unknown and we don't always know what to expect. Be present with yourself and those around you. Stop thinking of the past and worrying about the future. You will be okay, and life will carry us onward. I have beckoned harmony into my life and so can you.

I will leave you with this note: *"Be ever mindful. Be ever willing to move on. Be ever creative. Be ever true to yourself."*

Keri Lynn Powe is a talented, intuitive vivacious woman. She resides in Tennessee with her 17-year-old son Clayton. Keri is a beach loving hippie from Gulf Breeze, FL. She loves to travel and is most fond of the beautiful beaches of Kauai, HI. When not traveling, Keri enjoys working out, meditating, and studying bourbons and whiskeys.

Keri is a Master Massage Therapist with 11+years of massage/bodywork. Her intuition and loving spirit enhance her healing massages. She is passionate about learning the body/mind/soul connections. This has led her on a life journey of healing and growth as she has dealt with various traumatic events in her life. Her hope is to help provide tools for others to enrich and love their lives to the fullest.

Keri Powe

Master Massage Therapist

"We are all broken.
That's how the light gets in."
- Ernest Hemingway

Prolific Self Love

Feeling hurried and fearful, I moved quickly so I didn't get caught. Sneaking cautiously into my room, I sat on the cold linoleum flooring next to my bed, where I could quickly hide what I was doing from my parents. The brown paper bag crackled as I tucked the book inside and wrapped it. I had never wrapped a present before. Happily, I put the present in my backpack and headed off to school. I have been invited numerous times to birthday parties but have never been allowed to go. All my school friends knew I was a "Jehovah's Witness" and celebrating birthdays were not acceptable in our religion. But I was going to this one! I was in the 5th grade and it was my best friend's birthday party at ShowBiz

Pizza. I had figured out a plan and I was absolutely going to enjoy giving her a present!

After school, on the car ride to Show Biz, I sat in wonderment as to what would happen next. I could barely contain my excitement. To be able to give a gift would be wonderful for me! I had never given a gift. I experienced for the first time so much happiness and delight knowing I gave somebody a gift and they were going to open what I had wrapped with my love.

Then, flashes of my parents walking in and seeing me at a birthday party! Yikes! I would for sure get yelled at and snatched out of there. How embarrassing it would be! Disobeying Jehovah and my parents meant punishment and guilt. Those thoughts quickly disappeared as we walked into the glitzy, fun-filled ShowBiz Pizza with flashing lights, loud noises of children screaming in excitement, bells and whistles from the video games, and the delicious smell of pizza and cotton candy! I couldn't help feeling a little socially weird, not knowing what goes on at birthday parties.

It had been explained there were two reasons why we do not celebrate birthdays. One: there are only two birthdays talked about in the Bible and both ended in murder/beheadings.

The second reason is birthdays give excessive honor and glory to an individual. Believing if we give honor to an individual, we are worshipping that person and taking glory away from God. However, there were no murders or beheadings at this birthday party. There was jubilation singing happy birthday and eating birthday cake. The best part was opening gifts! I could not wait for her to open my gift! It was only a book, but I didn't care. It was the first gift I had ever given! My gift was the last to be opened because of the plain brown paper bag I had used. They did not realize it was a gift. This made me feel a twinge of embarrassment and shame. None the less, I shouted excitedly, "Happy Birthday!" It felt like an explosive gasp of air bursting out as I said words I've never said before. This was my very first expression of freedom and what it felt like to give. Looking back, I realize how good I felt giving a present and seeing the happy surprised reaction on her face as she opened her gifts. I wouldn't understand what this freedom of giving did for me until later on in life. It was, for sure, a starting catalyst for me to rebel in order to listen to my intuition.

My parents would never find out I went to the birthday party. I was a sweet and obedient child on

the outside. Like most children, I had a need for the
taste of rebellious adventure. Despite that, I was
fearful of my parents' discipline and Jehovah's
destruction, plus losing the opportunity to be on a
'paradise earth', if I disobeyed. From an early age, I
had to defend my faith as a Jehovah's witness.
Starting in kindergarten, my parents conditioned me
to stand up for "myself"and my faith to my God. On
the first day of school, every year, I was not allowed
to stand for the Pledge of Allegiance, put my hand
over my heart and say the pledge. Rather, I was to
"stand and pledge my allegiance to Jehovah only",
silently, to not bring attention to myself. I remember
sitting on the sidelines of the classroom or being
sent to the library, while holiday celebrations and
birthdays were going on, wishing I could participate
in the festivities. I learned social distancing before it
was a thing. Growing up Jehovah's Witness was
stifling and controlling at times. We didn't celebrate
ANY holiday, not even Christmas! It was a rarity but
a few times we would go to our non JW families the
day after Christmas. We would eat leftover
Christmas dinner. My parents would deny our
Christmas gifts from family. This left me feeling out
of place. Often not knowing how to accept gifts left
me feeling needy when I did receive gifts. Shunned
and shunning outsiders because they didn't believe as

we did. The hurt feelings of loved ones who didn't understand the religion.

On the car ride home, there would be a lecture on why we do not celebrate the holidays. "Christmas is a lie and it's not really Jesus Christ's birthday" and "We do not celebrate birthdays because it does not honor God or could end in a beheading!" If we committed a sin, we would be shamed by having to confess our "sins" to the elder men of the congregation. Disfellowshipping or shunning from the congregation is another form of their religious "punishments" to those who are disobedient of the man-made rules and indoctrinations of the religion. Cut off from all communication and association with your JW family and friends. I never really got to know my grandparents, aunts, uncles, or cousins. "Unbelievers" or "worldly people" were commonly known as "people who are of Satan's world". Yes, even family members! Why would I need to? I had Jehovah and his organization as my family. *Eye roll* "Bad association spoils useful habits" and "a friend of the world is an enemy of God" were common sayings when I wanted to spend time with non JW family or friends from school. No sports, school dances, or team school spirit/politics. Religious politics can make anyone feel guilt that's heavy and suppressive from being a sinner. Fast forward to my 20's. My rebellious attitude got me disfellowshipped. I had to rewire my thoughts and address some of my ruminating negative thoughts and limitations. After going through a divorce and raising a child as a single parent, I felt as though I was always doing something wrong. Negative repetitive thinking can be soul draining. Failures, such as divorce, tend to stick in our mind as a punishment or a negative thought process. I stayed in a dark mental attitude for a while. A few years later, my intuition would tell me to go back to religion.

I was guided back to practicing as a JW, along with my two sons and my second husband, all who were new to the faith. My husband felt this religion fit his beliefs and lifestyle for the time being, as JW's offered *Free Home Bible Study*. I had a new outlook on life, going back to my faith as a JW, now that I was an adult. I felt I could be one successfully. We made progress slowly, as there are many "high standards of living" as a JW. During this time, I went back to school to become a massage therapist to help support our family. I had always wanted to be a massage therapist since I was 12! It was at massage school I would learn of Louise Hay. A classmate I became close friends with, introduced me to Louise

Hay's affirmations. She told me how deserving I was of some good news I had received. She was genuinely excited and happy for me. No one had ever told me I was deserving of something good. Until this point, I had it ingrained into me I was not worthy of anything good. Within the JW'S bible scriptures translation, in Romans, it talks about God's undeserved kindness in conjunction with sin. However, most widely used bibles use the word grace. God's grace holds a warm, loving feeling. Undeserved kindness feels restrictive and takes away the depth of love God truly has for us. This was a huge epiphany for me! God's grace allows space for forgiveness and deep unconditional love. Louise's affirmations were full of love, grace, and kindness to warm my soul. In her book, *Experience Your Good Now!*, I learned more about affirmations. Affirmations are thoughts you think and words you speak, including your internal dialogue/self-talk. Typically, they are negative-based thoughts and ideas from what was instilled in us at a young age. Whether it's religious, work, military, political, or physical appearances, good or bad, these thoughts are always there. Negative thoughts do not feel good. They make you feel judgmental, angry, and depressed. I wanted to feel good! Louise taught me positive patterns of thinking and speaking. She explained, "Affirmations are like planting seeds in the ground. First, they germinate, then they shoot up through the ground. It takes some time to go from a seed to a full-grown plant. And so it is with affirmations - it takes some time from the first declaration to the final demonstration. Be patient." It takes time, self-love and grace when changing thought patterns. What I discovered while learning new positive affirmations was, how much and often I was saying negative affirmations! I was so embarrassed of my own negative self-talk. I had to actively replace each negative thought with a positive one, rewiring my brain to be positive. Starting out with just trying not to complain for one whole 24-hour day. This forced me to rewire my thoughts and feelings on how I looked at life and myself. The first affirmation I started with was "All is well, all is good, and everything is working out to my highest power." This replaced my "I hate everything, and everything sucks" affirmation. From these positive affirmations, I knew I wanted to change how I lived my life in my head and talked to myself. I wanted to love myself and my life! I wanted to help my husband and sons to be positive too. Like a lot of people, I was not taught self-love. Self-love for me is allowing myself grace and being easy and kind to myself when I need to be.

Furthering my studies in massage, I was guided to Hawaii for a retreat in 2011 to study and train with Hawaiian Kumus (teachers). I studied the healing wisdom of Hawaiian Lomilomi massage, along with Hawaiian culture and history. Little did I realize, this was the beginning of my great awakening. I cannot put words to what changed me on this island of Kauai. Kauai is known as the "Garden Isle". The warmest of embraces as you walk into the fragrant dewy island. As if you walked into your grandmother's kitchen while she's cooking. Close your eyes and imagine the sweetest fragrant smells of tropical flowers, and pleasant sounds of birds, waterfalls plus the lull of beautiful mellow Hawaiian music. You can feel the Aloha spirit, even in the sparkle of the residents' smiling eyes. Kauai is paradise!!! The only litter you see is the lovely petals of local wildflowers. It's filled to the brim with the Aloha spirit, a love beyond what I've ever known. Lomilomi goes beyond "massage". It's spirit showed me how incredibly wonderful and beautiful I am. Prolific self-love. This internal, sweet self-love is on another level, a deep love, like the love for your favorite person or pet. Freedom from self-hatred. Seeing the beauty in my flaws. It was an incredible experience of healing. Ancient traditions create balance and harmony with your true identity past, present, and future, as well as the art of forgiveness and compassion. Ineffable. During a group discussion at the retreat, one of the teachers told me to get ready for a big life change. I had no idea what was meant by that until nine months later. July 2012 my husband, who was thirty-two years old, died of a ruptured aneurysm in his heart.

I was thirty-five years old when this most devastating event I had ever experienced happened. Prior to my husband's death, he was battling an addiction and needed to get help. During an unexpected hospital visit, it was revealed that he had a large aneurysm on his aorta. Not life threatening at the moment, but it needed to be taken care of within a few months. I was terrified. I felt powerless! There was no easy fix for this. The doctors wouldn't operate until he got his addictions under control, to avoid further complications. The only way he could do that was by going to rehab. The JW's shun those who have drug and alcohol addictions because it looks bad on their organization. They thought it would be best for him to be disfellowshipped/ shunned, so he could get his own outside help and clean up his act! Rehab provided some much-needed family counseling for all of us. Gary and I grew even closer to each other. We had been together for

thirteen years at this point. I felt a greater bond with
our relationship despite the situation. We studied
addiction and codependency. Codependency is a
physiological condition or relationship where a
person/caregiver is affected by another person who is
an addict. It's an interesting side effect of addiction.
When addressed through therapy, it is revealed
codependency is deeply rooted in feelings from
childhood of hurt, loss, and anger. My understanding
of codependency has helped me identify a lot of
learned undesirable, unhealthy behaviors and
affirmations surrounding things out of my control.
Three weeks into rehab, I got a call that my husband
was being rushed to the hospital. When my son and
I arrived, we were brought into a private room to be
told my husband, my son's father, had died. I wailed
and wailed. All the breath went out of me. A flood
of emotions and tears. As some may know, moments
after a death the world becomes surreal. There was
no time for emotions.

No one and nothing can ever prepare you for the
death of a loved one. Planning the funeral is like
planning a morbid wedding. Picking out his clothes
for the funeral. Sifting through songs ... getting lost
in the words. Making the arrangements at the
funeral home. Decisions I never ever thought I'd

have to make, all within a couple of days. Gathering
his belongings from the rehab. Trying to figure out
what really happened at his death. Not to mention,
he died in a rehab and the speculation which goes
along with it. All the negative talk and fear came
back into my head. It felt as though my whole world
crumbled and came crashing down! Grief and
sorrow filled my soul. We had worked so hard to
understand his addiction. We were making so much
progress in our own relationship with ourselves! All
of which were helping with our relationship as a
family. A few months later, some tasteless things
were said within the JW congregation about my
husband's death. This made me think real deep about
love and how God treats us when we are feeling
down in our life. I did not feel loved or genuine love
in this religion. It felt a lot more like conditional love
in order to gain *their* approval, rather than God's
love. I wanted no part of it anymore. What I had
learned about love through positive affirmations and
loving myself without judgment did not line up with
what this religion taught. I learned more about love
using affirmations than I ever learned from studying
the bible. Realizing this, I started awakening little by
little over time. Awakenings allow freedom. Freedom
to enjoy life without judgment. I slowly faded away
from practicing as a JW. Further adjustments had to

be done to my thinking and affirmations once again. It was at this time I watched *The Secret*, learning about the Law of Attraction (LoA). LoA is a fast track to rewiring your thoughts. In my opinion, it is based on love and gratitude. I'm down with that! This is where I belong. Which is really no physical place, but this is where my soul resides: love and gratitude. It can't be disputed. LoA is a lifestyle thought by thought. "Manifesting" my life was a hard concept to understand. Especially as I was about to find out more horrible news. A year and a half after my husband died, I got a phone call from my oldest son's therapist. My son, 16, had been living with his dad for the past five years. The therapist explained to me he had shot and killed his dad. My first-born, who I breast fed as a baby, and cared for until he was eleven. Who I allowed to be free to have a relationship with his dad. I was crushed to my soul once again. You see, his dad was mentally abusive and there were also reports of some physical abuse. This is not a reason to ever take the life of someone. My son was charged as an adult with a life sentence 30+ years. Who saw that coming?!? I didn't! Hadn't my younger son and I been through enough already?? This was a lot to process, especially after my husband's death. Did I manifest this? For some time I questioned everything to do with God, the

Universe, and even myself. I was overly cautious of every thought. Anxiety and depression set in. I knew in order for my sons to have self-love and awareness, I would have to teach them by how I talked to them and myself, as I was never taught this. The first time I saw my oldest son, after he was locked up, was difficult and surreal. How do you even know how to feel when your own child has taken someone's life? I also understood this was not my fault nor a choice I made. He was extremely remorseful. He knew what he did, and of course knew it was wrong … plus knowing he'd be in prison for a long time. He would not talk about it any further, nor did I want to hear anything more of what happened. I will never forget when I asked if he was doing okay being locked up. He said, "Yes, Mom. They treat me better here than Dad ever treated me." That said it all to me of why he did it. From that day forward, I promised to empower him with love and grace. I still have no idea to what extent his dad abused him. It breaks my heart he's locked up because of how his dad treated him and his resolution was murder. Having a child locked up is an ongoing healing wound. I know I have lots more healing to do surrounding my son.

I continue to learn and grow on my spiritual journey. I started meditation and yoga practices.

Meditation did not come easy for me. It takes loving dedication to yourself to *listen* to your breath. Starting out with yoga, I learned how to turn my focus to myself how to use my breath to move into the next pose and space, or asana. I love yoga movements because they are based on what you can do, not on what you should do. It pushes you to your threshold and lovingly reminds you to give yourself a deep breath. We can do anything, even if it's just standing and breathing. That's yoga. The more you practice, the more you can do. Meditation goes even deeper. To maintain focus on just your breath, without the mind wandering 5 trillion times is daunting. It can be done, even if it's just second by second, to slowly clear all the monkey mind chatter. There are countless meditation videos to help guide you. I started with doing short 3- to 5-minute guided meditations. Most importantly, what I have learned is there's no wrong way to meditate. If you are taking the time to focus and be aware of your breath, for even one full breath, that's great! Just like the waves of life, so is my meditation practice. Most recently, I've tried Kundalini yoga. It is one of my favorites for breathwork meditation with mantras and movement, or kriyas. Mantra, translated from Sanskrit, means 'tool for the mind'. Mantras are word sound vibrations which help you to focus

mindfully. Aum or Om are the most common
mantras as they hold universal meaning to be the
sound of the creation of the universe. I include the
use of positive affirmations as mantras. I even go as
far as writing them on my mirrors in my bathroom
and bedroom, constant happy reminders to love life.
They make me smile and feel good. I have gained
deep insights and inspiration from Louise Hay and
LoA, my Hawaiian teachers, and others on a journey
similar to mine. It has guided me on an excursion to
finding the light path of love. Love lights up
darkness. Changing my whole outlook and thought
pattern was very challenging. Even now, I am still
working on it every day. There's a depth of
knowledge in learning how to let go of old negative
patterns. As we continue to see the world change, to
be able to just observe with love rather than
participate in the rhetoric is a huge step in self-love
and love towards others. Allowing myself to be
gentle and kind to myself during this process, not
beating myself up because I didn't do things this way
or that, or because I was having negative thoughts
again is part of self-love. One of my favorite sayings
I learned and live by daily, is from my Hawaiian
retreat, "What anyone thinks of me is none of my
business." This is the complete opposite thinking I

grew up with when thinking of others. It helped me to move forward to do what's best for me and my son. Not to be held back by what other others think I should be doing. Knowing the Universe loves and supports me always.

The traumas endured in my life made me evaluate how my thoughts create my reality. Religion taught me everything bad happens to me because I'm a sinner and my sinful thoughts. Spirituality taught me how to rid myself of thinking like a sinner, and how to think like a lover. The word prolific means producing abundant growth or reproduction, fruitful. So, having prolific self-love feels like sweet face kisses from a baby or happy puppy, just pure happiness and joy! It's the sweetest essence of life. Through continued rewiring of my thoughts, I am able to navigate successfully through life.

Phyllis was born and raised in New York City. She has worked in corporate treasury for over twenty years. Most of her career has been spent in various genres of entertainment where she worked for cable networks, recording artists and Broadway production companies. She earned her Master's Degree in Media Studies & Media Management from the New School University in Greenwich Village.

She is an intuitive and Empath who shares her gifts with friends and loved ones. This year she also became a certified Reiki One healer and plans to continue her certification in Level Two. Her dream is to one day own a conscious living crystal store and center where customers can sit around the grounds and take in the beauty of nature, a meditation/classroom to expand knowledge as well as a labyrinth for people to walk and receive Divine guidance. And to live on acres of land where she can grow a vegetable garden.

Phyllis lives in suburban New Jersey close to the back roads she loves so much where she rides her black and pink Harley. She continues to enjoy going to rock concerts and following her favorite New York sports teams - the New York Rangers and New York Yankees.

When she isn't riding, traveling or working she loves to cook and garden. Currently she is working on a cookbook, taking family recipes and putting a healthy spin on them.

Phyllis
Lamattina

"When you get clear about your heart's desire, the Universe steps up in magnificent ways to support you!"

– HeatherAsh Amara

On the Outside
Looking (With)In

I look around the classroom, in Greenwich Village,
New York City at the other eight students sitting in
a circle listening intently to the professor. I wonder
to myself, "What the hell am I doing here?" I feel
like an outsider. I am in my late thirties, clearly older
than the rest of the graduate students, perhaps even
the instructor. My insecurity of being the eldest
student is abruptly cut short as the instructor
describes the requirements of the course. I am truly
out of my comfort zone. Panic and hot flashes take
over my body as I listen to the description of the
class, titled *Exploratory Film*.

My mind and heart race, my palms sweaty, as I wonder how I am going to deal with this insanity in my last semester of graduate school. Muriel, the professor, is an aging valley girl and performance artist. Her speech pattern is filled with long drawn out syllables and she says, "like" often, reminding me of the actress Sarah Bernhardt. She turns off the classroom lights and shows a clip from a short film called "Bouncing Balls." Once I hear the title, I relax as I imagine it's about colorful, bouncing rubber balls and children giggling. Negative. Instead, it was a naked man shot in black and white, holding his penis against his torso with one hand, while cupping and bouncing his testicles with the other. I gasped silently. What..... The ....!!!

In shock, I took a deep breath to calm myself. My intuition involuntarily took over as I heard my inner voice say, "Think like the professor. You'll be fine." So, in the coming weeks, I did exactly that. I tried to think of what would impress this Bohemian, Avant-Garde artist.

Gone was my linear, mainstream thought process. Cue in large doses of creativity that had no boundaries! As the semester passed, I created video projects titled *Ovulation* and *Sex Text*. I got an A in the course. My intuition was right again!

Ever since I could remember, I have been nudged by intuition and had premonitions. As a young child, I felt I was different. I was shy, loved to read and devoured books about science, especially geology and astronomy. I was intrigued by astrology and found it fascinating how the placement of the planets had something to do with personality traits. I had thoughts, which came true often. I didn't know this was called manifestation.

As a child, I lacked self-confidence and simply wanted to fit in. I was born to be different and one to not blend into the crowd. I always knew intuitively my soul had a purpose and fitting in was not part of the plan. My intuition was constantly on high alert, and my gut instincts helped save me from many teenage shenanigans. Most recently, I learned being extremely sensitive and introverted are characteristics of an empath. An empath is described as having the ability to feel and experience other individual's emotions and sensitive to loud noise. Do you have any idea how annoying it is to live with a loud Italian-American family?

Did you ever have a closeness to God, even if not practicing a religion, per se?

Growing up in a Catholic grammar school, there was an uncanny and ever-present sense of spirituality I didn't quite understand until later in life.

Now imagine me as a teen, hair teased high, attitude as big as my hair. I only wanted to be cool. Concerts gave me a sense of belonging and I loved rock music, especially being part of the counterculture of the 80's heavy metal scene and sporting a leather jacket. My confidence was blossoming because I had my first sense of community amongst like-minded individuals. Music was our connection.

In 1999, I was really tested by the Universe. I wholeheartedly relied on my intuition and relationship with God to guide me through the next two years. I was diagnosed with Lyme Disease after several months of misdiagnosis. No matter how much or little I slept, I was eternally fatigued. According to the internet, it could have been leukemia, lupus or something much worse. My inner voice guided me to find the right rheumatologist after screening several doctors. My treatment was balanced with both Eastern and Western Medicine protocols. The doctor also cut gluten, sugar, and dairy from my diet. I was so relieved I chose this doctor as my medical professional. Part of the treatment meant a long time confined to bed. It was during this period I made a list of things I wanted to accomplish when I recovered. At the top of the list was earning my master's degree in media & film. I loved taking videos and still photography through my young adult years as a hobby. Having worked in entertainment finance for years, I needed to cultivate my creative side. I enrolled in graduate school shortly after my recovery while working full time as a finance executive.

During treatment, I prayed a lot. The lessons I learned throughout the experience would provide the foundation which would be used from that moment on to live a more peace-filled, happy life.

I found a learn-how-to-meditate kit in the bargain section of Barnes & Noble, my first introduction to mantras and meditation. The book and cassette tapes (pre-YouTube) gave me insight into something that provided the peace I had been longing for throughout my life.

I learned stillness through the new meditation practice. It helped heal my body from the wretched disease and the effects of the harsh treatment. I had an IV of antibiotics, was given weekly injections of penicillin, and was taking oral malaria medication.

This toxic cocktail coupled with the disease created havoc on me. I was a mess, physically and mentally. My hair fell out, my brain felt like an unsolved jigsaw puzzle, and I had no energy. I often described the disease as PMS, the flu and a nervous breakdown all rolled into one. The weekly intravenous vitamin infusions my doctor gave me provided an energy reprieve for a day or so, and that is what kept me going.

It was the meditation practice which helped calm and still my mind and emotions, getting me through the endless harsh days and nights.

As I healed, I read about Buddhism and the wisdom of Deepak Chopra even though reading was challenging as my brain had a hard time processing information. Deepak's book, *Perfect Health*, was my first introduction to Ayurveda, the traditional Indian principles of balance of the body using diet, breathing and herbs. Its literal translation means "Science of Life." I took a dosha quiz (an Ayurveda body type quiz) to discover my body type, and the accuracy was incredible. I decided to incorporate some of the suggestions of foods into my diet.

Understand this Catholic girl didn't know much about Buddhism. The Merriam-Webster dictionary defines the religion as: "Buddhists believe that suffering is inherent in life and that one can be liberated from it by cultivating wisdom, virtue, and concentration." The mindfulness described by Buddhists resonated with me, and I became curious about it.

Once fully recovered from the Lyme, I continued this lifestyle. I discovered the woman I worked with was a practicing Buddhist. She and I became very friendly. She was the light in an otherwise dark department of the media organization where we worked. We were having a really bad day. I responded to someone who was balking at me in a calm manner, while providing a solution to the issue at hand. She came into my office and asked, "Do you practice Buddhism too?" I told her I was raised Catholic and had recently become curious about Buddhism and read up on it while recovering from Lyme. She invited me to go to her temple after work one evening. I was so grateful to be introduced to an evening of chanting and mindfulness, and while this happened almost two decades ago, I can define it as one of the moments that changed my spiritual path. The large room was filled with about a hundred people. Pleasantries were exchanged along with hugs and smiles. The room became silent and everyone held their malas. Malas are a string of 108 prayer beads to count the number of times you say the mantra (verse). They are similar to rosary beads as it helps the person stay focused on reciting the mantra. After chanting the mantra, "Nam myoho renge kyo" 108 times, I left the temple filled with incredible inner peace.

Before any of this, I only knew prayers to the Lord and Mother Mary, which I still pray daily.

However, I currently believe there is no one definitive way to pray to the Divine and ascended masters. Shortly after my evening at the temple, I signed up for Transcendental Meditation (TM) classes and learned how to formally meditate. TM is extremely easy. You can Google how to do it now. Back in the day, you had to pay thousands of dollars to learn the technique. A Sanskrit mantra or word is repeated over and over for twenty minutes.

As the years flew by and the Lyme was in the rearview mirror, I read more about living consciously. I was introduced to Hay House Radio, Tosha Silver, Eckhart Tolle, Dr. Christiane Northrup and Gabby Bernstein to name a few. All of these experts in their respective discipline gave me various methodologies as well as incredible information to cultivate my new lifestyle. I learned about manifestation, eating healthy, new year rituals to bring in abundance and much more. I was a much happier person. I even bought myself a black and pink Harley Davidson motorcycle. It was another thing checked off of the bucket list I had created years ago. The biker community was another demographic I felt a sense of kinship. The sense of community from the biker and music worlds fed my soul.

It wasn't long when another life lesson took place. Due to unforeseen circumstances, I moved to Florida to stay with my parents. I was living a Seinfeld episode, complete with Uncle Morty and Del Boca Vista! This was a time of extreme disappointment and sadness for me. On the drive down I-95 from New York to Florida, I had nineteen hours to contemplate the purpose of this journey. Along with the anger and confusion, I had a sense of peace and it won marginally in the battle in my head. Something kept telling me all would eventually be fine and this would be another breakthrough in life I needed.

Unlike Stella, though, I did NOT get my groove back where some call "paradise!" My thoughts focused on what I had left behind instead of what was present and upcoming. I didn't look at it as an adventure, but a loss. I was in mourning. I missed my friends, financial security, my home. All my belongings were in a storage room I left behind. I took with me only the necessities: some clothes, my laptop, a favorite pillow and whatever small comforts that would squeeze into the back seat of my car.

After six months of financial consulting work, traveling to Georgia and central Florida, I was back at my parents' house in the guest room full time. As grateful as I was for having a home and family to go to, it was exceedingly difficult for me and for them as well. We were in each other's way. They were not used to their adult child living at home. I certainly wasn't used to having "roommates!" I decided the factor to making this experience tolerable would be my attitude. I needed to collect my ammunition of mantras, affirmations, prayer, and books which I had and tap back into a daily meditation and prayer practice. This was the most difficult part of the journey. Always sassy and full of snark, I needed to tone it down. How do you find the silver lining of moving in with your elderly parents who empty the dishwasher at 7am when you are trying to sleep? What was the purpose? These questions interrupted my peace daily.

My brother, who lived close by, would foster great conversations about God and surrender with me. His favorite saying is, "Let Jesus take the wheel." As much as I tried, surrendering was a challenging process for me. Patience is not one of my virtues. However, I knew I had to trust the journey, use what I had learned throughout the years to maintain my inner peace and most of all enjoy this precious time with family. In my heart I knew it was temporary, even though I was scared. The saying, "You can't have fear if you have faith," was also hard to embrace. I had nothing to lose. Each day gave me a fresh opportunity to surrender a bit more, to embrace my new life. I slowly did, one day at a time.

As I loved to cook, Mom's kitchen became my sanctuary. I frequently gave her a break and prepared healthy meals for my family. My brother would join us, and sitting around the dinner table together gave me great comfort. I embraced my daily morning prayer and meditation practice. Every day my shoulders loosened up a bit more. Soon, they weren't attached to my ears as they had been when I arrived!

One afternoon, I was out riding the Harley and passed a store, a tiny yellow building with a sand and gravel parking lot. The sign indicated it was a crystal store. I made a mental note of where it was. On my next ride to the area, I decided to go in. The incredible, positive energy when I entered the store was palpable, as the bells on the door handle shook and alerted the staff someone arrived. The smell of lavender, patchouli, sage, and other unidentifiable scents were soothing, the staff warm and welcoming. Meditation music played softly in the background. Filling the room, sitting atop shelves lined with white lace, were colorful crystals in glass bowls, with paper slips describing the stones. There were small, tumbled gemstones in addition to floor to ceiling glass display cases filled with the more precious, larger crystals and quartz singing bowls. Chimes hung in a corner and another room was dedicated to books, candles, and sage. I felt happy here. As a little girl, I loved gemstones and crystals. I don't remember how, but I procured a yellow quartz when I was eight years old. I called it my lucky rock. I even gave it to my grandparents when they went to Italy that summer for good luck. To be in a store abundant with crystals filled my heart with joy!

After I purchased a few stones for my collection, the sweet salesperson placed a flyer in my bag. When I got home, I read the flyer and discovered they did a weekly meditation class. In an effort to meet like-minded people, I began attending the guided

meditation. Each week, I'd have a ritual: Chipotle for dinner, a visit to the crystal store to purchase a small stone, chat with the women who worked there, ending the evening with the meditation.
I made friends there, including the owner, another New Yorker.

Not too long after, the owner called and offered me a part-time job. I learned a great deal from the ladies here. I was a sponge, soaking up all the knowledge they had to offer about conscious living and being mindful. I was introduced to singing bowls, intention-setting, and new moon meditations. I thought to myself, I now found a third group of people I resonate with in life. Each of us had a different journey which brought us to this store. The Universe brought us together to learn and grow from one another.

The store carried an array of books about crystals, Eastern philosophies, angels, and so much more. I bought many of them to learn further about concepts which were new to me like H'oponopono, the Hawaiian mantras of forgiveness, and how to expand my beliefs in the spiritual realm. This was an essential part of the breakthrough. It was a crash course in conscious living within six months. And the benefits that it provided to me were noticeable to many, including my own family.

It was within this period I began to receive messages during meditation. I knew then, I was on the right path. I am no stranger to messages from the other side. Years ago, after my maternal grandmother passed, she would wake me up at 1:10am a few nights per week.

Sometimes I felt someone pushing my arm before I woke. I knew it was her. The number 110 became her sign repeatedly. I knew it was her because it was her address for many years. I asked her to stop waking me up because I was scared, and she did. When living in Florida, I asked her to send me signs when I was awake. She definitely received MY message. I would see 110 on license plates, clocks, pages in a book, addresses - anything where numbers were involved, 110 showed up. It gave me such great comfort knowing she was with me. But the voices I heard in my meditative state were of the Divine. They gave me messages of hope during this difficult time. I knew by surrendering my power to God, living consciously, and spending this unexpected time with my aging parents and brother was all part of God's plan and finding my soul's purpose. Once I surrendered and fully accepted my situation, that's when things began to shift. Calls from recruiters in New York scheduling phone interviews came out of nowhere for open positions. One recruiter even flew me up to New York after a call to see their client in person. By the time I got to the airport gate for my return flight to Florida, my phone rang with the job offer. I enthusiastically accepted. It worked! My shift in perspective, faith and letting go changed my life. It was a miracle. Now I know its co-creation with the Divine. All in God's time, not mine. Surrendering was a very essential component of the plan.

On the drive back to New York, I had two realizations. First, everything had to happen exactly as it did to make me the person who I was in that moment. The exact sequence of events had given me the breakthrough to live life in a state of gratitude, mindfulness and peace. I needed to lose everything to start over with a new perspective. It was the only way.

With the spiritual seeds planted back in 1999, I needed to cultivate these seeds by being humbled, (living with my parents,) working in a crystal store to learn more about conscious living, surrounded with like-minded people and time to devote to my spirituality. This was the formula to help me thrive.

Second, we truly can live on very few material things. Everything I needed for two years fit in the back seat of a car. I didn't need or miss anything that was in my storage room. The possessions seem so trivial now, as my discovery placed more importance on the moments with my family and the journey which enlightened me, rather than the quantity of my material belongings. As I unpacked my boxes from storage when I moved into my new apartment, I could not believe the collection of useless junk I had amassed over the years. I decided to donate a good portion of it to a veteran's organization. As my belongings decreased, my blessings and gratitude increased.

This breakthrough and shift has given me richer spiritual experiences. In recent years, I have received messages quite a few times during meditation. Mother Mary has been a guide for me on several of them. One morning during a meditation, I had a vision of her and the Lord. She looked up at the puffy, white clouds where Jesus appeared and said, "Lord, it's time." I came out of the meditation, sensing it was a warning. I got dressed and went to work. Later that day, I found out from a colleague via a phone call, my boss had hired my replacement and was using me until the new person could start later in the month. It was an extremely toxic environment, and I was looking for another job anyway. When I hung up the phone, I left the office and the deceit. I never returned. I was hired at my current job a short month later. Again, my intuition was screaming for me to leave that day, as well as signaling all would be well.

More recently, while meditating, I heard a voice say, "the church outside of Butte." I went to work and all through the day I kept hearing it. On my lunch hour, I Googled, "church outside Butte" (disclaimer - I have never been to Butte, Montana nor do I know anything about the state other than it has great roads to ride on). My Google search resulted in an incredible discovery. There is a church perched on top of a mountain, located on the Continental Divide with a 90-foot statue of Mother Mary, called Our Lady of the Rockies. It has been added to my bucket list as something is calling me to go there one day soon.

I found my Zen over the years and the freedom that would take me on the ride of my life.

Gratitude has become the focus of my life. It's a simple practice beginning with the birds singing, appreciating what I have, grateful I have a job and the tribe I attracted into my life. In the suburbs of New York City, I sit on my balcony, which has become my sanctuary and sacred space for prayer and meditation. Looking out over a bucolic, serene lake, the little rabbits hop across the grass as the sweet melodies of the birds sing to all each day. How did I miss this for so many years?

God truly embraced me and gave me a gift I prayed for all my life. I had to connect with my awesomeness and raise my awareness to live life in alignment with the Divine. That is when I realized I was never alone. Riding my Harley along the back roads of farmlands, I become awe inspired with the peacefulness of all of creation. Sure, I still blunder, however I always strive to be the best version of myself. I learned these lessons are about the detours we take in life to find the open roads of freedom. Then, to relax and enjoy the ride. I occasionally have to quiet my ego talking to me, surrender to the ride and remember, "It's not the destination, it's the journey."

Surrender is the breakthrough. It could be right around that sweeping curve where you feel like you may fall off. Hold on for the ride of your life.

"Reaching for the you that exists beyond all the drama is what the spiritual search is all about."

- The Afterlife of Billy Fingers
... a true story by Annie Kagan

Felicia Brown is the co-founder of the Impromptu Rubber Duck Regatta (IRDR) and best-selling author of seven books. She is also a contributing author for several other books and has written for many national publications.

A massage therapist and entrepreneur since 1994, Felicia owns A to Zen Massage, an award-winning wellness spa in Greensboro, NC and speaks on many topics related to business, marketing, professionalism, empowerment and self-care at events around the globe and online. As one who loves to educate others, Felicia previously hosted the Pre-Conference Broadcast Series for One Concept Radio, interviewing massage, chiropractic and wellness educators.

Felicia works with select individuals and companies needing targeted motivation, creative empowerment, and thoughtful guidance to achieve their personal and professional goals. Her unique blend of innovative problem solving, entrepreneurial spirit and heart-centered coaching creates a custom experience for each client.

A native of North Carolina, Felicia and her husband David make their home near Greensboro. When not racing rubber ducks or conquering the world, she also loves reading, running, kayaking and doing yoga whenever possible.

Connect with Felicia and the IRDR at www.FeliciaBrown.com or Felicia@Spalutions.com.

Facebook: @FeliciaBrownLMBT @feliciabrownauthor @ImpromptuRubberDuckRegatta

https://www.facebook.com/groups/ ImpromptuRubberDuckRegatta

Instagram: @felicia_brown_author/ @imprompturubberduckregatta/

Linked In: https://www.linkedin.com/in/feliciaebrown/

Felicia Brown

Author, Licensed Massage Therapist,
Massage Educator and Marketer

*"A person shouldn't look too
far down her nose at absurdities.
Look at me. I dived right into one
absurd thing after another,
and here I am…
I wake up to wonder every day."*

- Lily Owens in *The Secret Life of Bees*
by Sue Monk Kidd

Quacking Up

Lying in bed one Sunday shortly after Easter, I felt clouded in sorrow and hopeless about the future. I had stayed under the covers until afternoon. In between naps, I spent time writing in my journal and scrolling Facebook. All to avoid the outside world. A lot had brought me down over the last few weeks, and it felt like I was sinking deeper by the day. I didn't want to stay here and needed my life back, or at least to feel happy enough to enjoy the sunshine. Instead, I was stuck in a murky, mucky darkness.

Over the last thirty-plus years, my life has largely been about business and making my mark in the world. To be blunt, I am an over-achiever, workaholic, and Type-A personality. The one who gets things done. A serial entrepreneur. A woman who wears many hats. I have been like this since I got my first job at age fourteen, maybe before then too.

It may seem unusual I brought these traits and skills to the field of massage therapy, but they helped propel me to own and manage several successful spas. While it's true I *love* to help people relax and unwind, and enjoy receiving massages as often as possible, my "work, work, work" drive and persona has remained and gotten stronger.

Over the years, I've endured periods of forced rest because my body broke down, got sick, or stopped functioning in such a way I had to STOP and recover. Some of these times have been accompanied by anxiety or depression, two "companions" I've dealt with all my life. Even with them in the mix, I have always bounced back, reset my course, gotten back to work - and my overachieving.

Nearly two months before my extended sleep-in, I'd spent several tension-filled weeks of investigation, meditation, and deliberation. An invisible yet powerful force – a sometimes deadly virus – was spreading quickly across the globe, leaving a trail of chaos and destruction all around. Then, in what felt like an instant, the world around me came to a screeching halt as businesses left and right shut down for safety, including my spa. After sending my staff home for an unplanned "spring break," I felt like I'd been gutted, left to bleed out while pondering a seemingly bleak future.

As a tenacious problem solver, I could not allow myself space to rest. Instead, I drove myself crazy trying to control the trajectory of my life. Some days were filled with hours of reading, researching and relaying information about community resources, unemployment and sanitation to staff and colleagues. Time eroded as I watched overlapping news programs, hoping to find solutions no one else had. I thought if I worked hard enough, read enough, worried enough, I could MAKE SOMETHING HAPPEN - as if I alone had the power to change the outcomes of this global issue and make sure everyone was okay.

Other times I was frozen with fear, overwhelmed by a surfeit of negative possibilities. What if one of us got sick or died? What if I never gave another massage or saw my beloved clients again? How would my husband and I – and my business – pay our bills? What if we lost our home, went bankrupt or became homeless? I was drowning in a sea of fear and grief.

Despite years of being physically active as a runner, triathlete, and yoga enthusiast, I also stopped working out for the most part. The solitude exercising created opened my heart and gave space for me to uncover realities too painful to face. Though I knew moving my body had many physical benefits, I didn't dare let in any more sadness.

I lost myself in whatever moments of escape I could find. From standing in a hot shower until the water ran cold to wrestling jigsaw puzzles while devouring bowls of ice cream, I did whatever I could to keep from breaking down. Often awake into the wee hours of the morning, I found no shame in utilizing my healthy supply of Xanax.

In the mornings, once I was able to peel myself out of bed, I'd wander around the yard talking to the budding wildflowers. Despite all the crap going on in the world, tiny plants were blooming en masse in the early spring. The colorful posies gave me the teensiest bit of hope to cling to. Then one day my husband had the grass cut, and most of my precious beauties were shredded. I'd begged him not to destroy this small piece of happiness I'd found, but he believed it more important to prevent rodents and ticks from invading.

"The yard guys are beheading all the wildflowers! How could you ask them to murder my friends?!! Why?!!" Sobbing and struggling to breathe, I collapsed on the couch, a heap of anguish.

My husband put his arms around me, trying his best to calm me down and justify his poorly timed decision. As I laid there crying, the pain, loss and grief of the proceeding weeks ripped through me like mower blades. Was I cracking up? That was uncertain, but I was by no means *okay*.

Sinking deeper into the sheets that spring morning, I knew some wildflowers had come back. Each day saw a few more returning, thriving again despite their setbacks. Thinking of them, a strategy I have used in times of anxiety or procrastination sprang to mind...Do ONE Thing. It's particularly helpful overcoming big challenges, especially if you aren't sure where to start, and breaks them into smaller manageable tasks.

When I'm feeling tired or unmotivated, I'll do ONE of the easiest or most familiar tasks first. Accomplishing something simple builds a sense of confidence and momentum, increasing energy for addressing bigger issues. When I'm rested and energized, I may start with the hardest thing. This allows worry and stress to dissipate, freeing up energy for other simpler items. Completing something challenging creates a huge sense of accomplishment.

Overcoming my despair and depression was not the same as reaching for a big goal. For weeks I'd been doing a lot of things to cope, but nothing was working well. Instead, I was getting worse. If only I could think of ONE thing I could do to move away from this dark, scary place and feel the smallest bit better…

Out of the blue, a warm, fuzzy memory floated into my mind. Several years prior, I was a speaker at an Orlando conference. One of several non-education events scheduled was a rubber duck race. I'd never seen anything like it and found the concept silly. However, many attendees were gleefully purchasing bright yellow competitors to raise money for charity and perhaps win a prize. Plastic bath toys didn't excite me much, but wanting to be a good sport, I bought an obligatory duck.

At race time, led by a large inflatable "momma duck," hundreds of canary-colored duckies glided down a "lazy river" to the floating finish line. A crowd gathered pool side to cheer on the yellow flock meandering along the man-made waterway. The competition was close initially, but halfway through, #128 broke away from the field, crossing the finish line first. Mildly disappointed my duck didn't win, I shrugged before moving on to another conference activity.

Later that evening, I gathered with friends for a dance party in the resort ballroom. Not long after our arrival, excited shouts and applause erupted as a duck-filled wagon rolled into the room. Immediately the event kicked into high gear. Party-goers surrounded the cart, passing ducks to everyone around the dance floor. Spots of yellow became twirling blurs as the little quackers found new perches on hats, in hair, even in underwear.

One mirthful duck lover climbed into the wagon and was pulled around the room like a Duck King on a traveling throne, a spontaneous conga line following behind. The cheerful golden flock infused the night and crowd with fun, merriment, and joy. What a precious memory!

As I recalled the glee of that evening, I wanted to go back in time and reconnect with the feelings of amusement and delight. Experiencing even a fraction of such frolic and freedom would be much better than I felt lying in bed.

Suddenly I had an idea for my ONE thing...

Besides wildflowers, there is a beautiful stream in my wooded yard. Cooper's Creek is both a backdrop for walks with my dogs and a setting for moments of reflection. When it rains, the creek grows from a trickle to a steady flow, and sometimes, a miniature rushing river. Whatever the water level, the lush greenery and gurgling waters provide an incredible escape when I need it. In the weeks before, I'd spent a lot of time watching the crystalline waters, staging several creek-side meditations. But on this day, I had an entirely different vision.

On the edge of my bathtub were two rubber ducks from the Florida race and others I'd collected since. Jumping out of bed and dressing, I walked into my bathroom, grabbing #489 – a three-and-a-half inch tall Classic Yellow Duck with sky blue eyes and bright orange beak (Quacky), and a two-and-a-half inch tall "unicorn-duck" with a pink beak, rainbow mane and tail (Uni).

Feeling nervous but hopeful, I gathered my courage as I walked downstairs into the kitchen.

"Will you go down to the creek with me for a rubber duck race?" I asked my husband.

Looking up from his tablet, he was confused. "A what?"

"A rubber duck race. I know it sounds silly, but I've done one before and think it will be fun. Please, let's go try it."

My husband is supportive of most everything I do, but is sometimes hesitant to make leaps into the unknown. His minimal enthusiasm about a duck race was not surprising, nor was the subtle eye roll following my request. I know he was quietly elated to see me dressed and motivated to do something beyond "sleep, scroll and cry" and wanted to make up for the recent wildflower execution. After a slight hesitation, he laced up his shoes and followed me outside.

As we walked through the woods to the creek, I imagined us laughing and cheering the ducks while they drifted around rocks and tree roots to the finish. We'd stand on the shore, clapping and whooping for the winner and runner-up. It was going to be great!

After establishing a finish line, I left my husband to hike through overgrown weeds to a launching spot at the top of the creek about a hundred feet away. I threw the ducks in together, eagerly anticipating waves of bliss to kick in.

Sadly, the water was far from rushing and was moving quite slowly. Without a current or a lazy river to push them, rubber ducks do not have much get up and go on their own. Thus, after the initial momentum at the start, Quacky and Uni floated in place for a few moments before drifting slightly downstream. There, they both got beached between rocks on the opposite bank, out of my reach. Now we had two DNFs (did not finish) and a rescue situation on our hands. My ONE thing was a disaster!

Feeling totally deflated and disappointed, my husband and I trudged back to the house. The fun race I'd imagined failed, leaving me feeling worse than before. Even so, I did not want to leave Quacky and Uni stranded nor waiting to be washed away into the lake beyond. Pouting, I grabbed a rake and stomped back alone to save them.

(*Author's note:* My husband did not suggest or condone abandoning the ducks.)

Though initially aggravated, the recon mission made me feel like I was back in summer camp, exploring the woods and trekking into the unknown. Tentative at first, I tiptoed across the slippery rocks, my confidence growing with each sandy step. Hiking past overgrown trees, winding vines and prickly bushes, my agility kicked in. Soon I was scaling the high creek bank, leaping from one rock to the next.

Armed with my garden-tool-turned-walking-stick, I fought off spider webs and loss of balance to become the brave heroine, rescuing the stranded racers from peril. Sweaty and satisfied, I was victorious in my quest and emerged from the woods, both grateful competitors in hand. Despite the disastrous race, and perhaps because of the obstacles, I got a delicious taste of the feelings I'd sought. My ONE thing was not what I envisioned, yet it lifted my spirits up higher than expected!

Realizing this, I reread part of an essay I'd seen a few weeks prior, by White Eagle, a Hopi elder:

"This moment humanity is going through can now be seen as a portal and as a hole. The decision to fall into the hole or go through the portal is up to you. If you repent of the problem and consume the news 24-hours a day, with little energy, nervous all the time, with pessimism, you will fall into the hole. But if you take this opportunity to look at yourself, rethink life and death, take care of yourself and others, you will cross the portal.

Don't feel guilty about being happy during this difficult time. You don't help at all by being sad and without energy. It helps if good things emanate from the Universe now. It is through joy that one resists. Also, when the storm passes, you will be very important in the reconstruction of this new world… What would you want to build for yourself? For now, this is what you can do: 'serenity in the storm.'"

Was holding the race and rescuing the ducks my first steps to climb out of the hole and into the portal? I wasn't sure, but I knew I felt better and was several strides closer to rediscovering joy.

After a rainstorm a few days later, my happiness exploded when my husband suggested we hold another race. Excitedly, I gathered Quacky, Uni and two more competitors: Little Red, a 2-inch tall power sprinter and Quicky, Quacky's younger brother.

Skipping back to the creek, I surprised myself with the level of enthusiasm I felt and decided to record the festivities for others to enjoy. Tapping into my confident stage persona and public speaking skills, I added unscripted pre-race commentary, unexpectedly giving the race an official name, the Impromptu Rubber Duck Regatta (IRDR).

The second event went well, producing more hilarity than predicted and living up to my initial vision. It seems all the years of watching the Tour de France and college basketball with my husband implanted in me an unknown ability to give live play-by-play and color commentary as racers floated by. The spring rains continued, bringing more races and a fifth challenger - MC Killer, a sleek Orca whale nearly four-and-a-half-inches from tip to tail.

A steady stream of ideas and inspiration followed, bringing the formation of "The Dream Team" the original five racers, and several new competitors. Race by race, I felt more energized, eagerly anticipating each event, and discovering untapped engagement and creativity. Still, I was not expecting the ducks to develop personalities, share their backgrounds, or reveal any "insider" secrets.

As a lifelong writer, I've had several experiences where words have flowed like #128 blazed across the lazy river finish line. Most often this happens when I'm out in nature, though it could be anywhere. Something captures my attention - a tree, a stone, a sunflower – and then, as if through headphones, a story spills into my mind. Flowing so quickly and distinctly different from other thoughts, I know these words are special and must find their way onto a page. When this happens, I stop what I'm doing to get everything on paper, even when it's about a rubber duck.

After a couple of disappointing races and one DNF, Uni disappeared for about a day, sparking concern and rumors of "foul play." We'd scoured our house top to bottom before finding him safe and alone in a quiet corner. Later, while running errands, I heard Uni's voice quietly emerge to share the story about why he went missing.

What came across immediately was Uni's love for the sport and his teammates. Quiet and introspective, Uni speaks with the swagger of a veteran NBA point guard but carries the pain of being an outsider on his sleeve. He's a unicorn in a duck's world, which is both an honor and a challenge. Uni's story spoke to me, and as I heard it unfold, I knew there was more to the IRDR and duck racing than fun and games.

A part of Uni's story, in his own words…

"I wasn't really missing. I just needed to disappear into myself for a while. It's hard to put into words...

The race Sunday started out awesome, you know. The course was really calm. It was just me and Big Yellow in a head-to-head match-up. We were both taking it easy in the beginning, knowing we'd probably sprint it out at the end.

And then BOOM! The rocks just came out of nowhere. I crashed into them and was paralyzed. I guess I was feeling a little cocky and not paying attention to what was happening. I know I finished ahead of Big Yellow, but I feel like my ego cost both of us the race."

Uni and I are a lot alike. We're both competitive leaders who take responsibility for problems out of our control and feel guilty when we can't fix everything. We're also reflective thinkers who need time alone to process our challenges and setbacks.

His shock at being stopped by the rocks – and not being able to perform at the high level he expected – had a striking parallel to my life's crash into the virus. Likewise, his disappearance and seclusion were similar, if shorter, to my recent isolation. In Uni's darkness, I saw my own, and in his return to racing after the setbacks, I glimpsed my life's eventual renewal.

Uni is not the only one to share his "thoughts" with me. At times, the ducks are insistent about when and where they want to speak out, though most often their wisdom and insights arrive mid-race or in our "interviews."

During a spontaneous practice session with Quacky, I'd forgone my rubber rain galoshes and was creek-side in hiking boots. He made a great first run, proving the surging course was safe for a formal event. At the finish line, I easily scooped Quacky up and launched him a second time. He made another quick finish but ended on the opposite bank, out of reach of my net. With fast waters threatening to sweep Quacky away, I reluctantly waded into the deep creek to save him.

Sloshing back to the house, "Expect the best, but wear your waterproof boots," echoed in my ears. As Quacky and I were alone in the woods, I knew it was he who had spoken. In that moment, I realized I was moving from cracking up to "quacking up" and giggled up the path.

The races and other duck-focused activities provide incredible bursts of freedom and creativity like I had when I was a young kid. Nothing makes me happier than doing something fun with or for the ducks. We've gone on field trips and photo shoots, planned recreational activities for their days off, and tried new sports. Recently I enrolled in a 200-hour Yoga Teacher Training and decided the ducks should learn too. I made custom yoga mats for the whole flock and set up a mini yoga studio before the program. Everyone took to the poses like ducks on water and are especially good at meditation!

All kidding aside, while Yoga Teacher Training was much different from the hustle bustle pace of duck racing, I think the courageous spirit of the ducks gave me strength and confidence to go "beak first" into the three-week intensive commitment. Beyond that, the Dream Team and all the quackers helped me rediscover my playful, spontaneous nature, something hidden away for years.

Unexpected outcomes continue. New opportunities to share what I've learned on this laugh- filled journey have opened, including this book and multiple speaking engagements. At first, I was hesitant to pass on "lessons from the ducks" for fear of detracting from my serious, professional persona, but no more. It seems what a duck wants, a duck gets!

Seven Tips for Quacking Up from The Dream Team

1) Every race is a great race. Be thankful for the things you often take for granted – the ability to

breathe, swim, quack and be on the planet.

2) Expect the best but wear your waterproof boots. Yes, all shoes can go in the water, but some shouldn't. Plan accordingly!

3) It's OK to look silly to find your joy. Most people are jealous THEY don't have the courage to be in the moment – or in the creek - with a bunch of rubber ducks.

4) Water is the best medicine. Even a small dose can cure a lot of what ails you, especially if you get your tail feathers wet!

5) Don't get stuck in the muck. We all have times where we feel lost, aimless, or caught on the rocks. But if you keep paddling, eventually you'll start moving in some direction and find your way to the finish line.

6) Embrace the rapids. While racing can be risky, holding yourself back from the thrills and spills of life can be much more damaging. Meet your challenges beak first and go for it!

7) The little things in life are the big things. I mean, look at us. We are only 2 to 3 inches tall and are changing the world.

As I reflect on the IRDR and the ducks, I'm in awe of the wisdom in and around me. If you're stuck in the muck like I was in the PD (pre-duck) era, consider trying ONE thing to make yourself move, laugh, or connect to a joyful memory. Take ONE step to bring a smile to your face or someone else's. Notice the unexpected or overlooked teachers around you. Most of all, listen to your inner quack, I mean, voice, and act on what it tells you.

You don't need to know the exact steps to try or where to look for answers. My story proves how a difficult moment in life created the opportunity to dive into the rapids beak first and keep paddling. Because of my challenges, I'm living more joyfully in the moment, and am definitely quacking up!

I was born in Los Angeles, California, however I was raised in Santa Maria on what was then the rural Central Coast. My love for the western lifestyle and horses flourished in this community where the most important function of the year was the Santa Maria Elk's Rodeo and Parade. Dad was a successful CPA and I was blessed to work with him for many years. Bookkeeping has been my livelihood for most of my adult life. The past few years the creative part of me is taking hold and this is something that comes naturally. My mom is an absolute genius with a sewing machine and my only daughter lives in Los Angeles, where she performs and writes stand-up comedy.

My obsession for "running with the wind" led me on a path of wildness, and my love for horses brought me to a new and deeper sense of my identity in recovery. Horses have been the constant in my life, and I hope I will never know the day it is my last one to ride. I have lived all over the state of California, alternating over the years with Washington and Oregon.

I now reside in Ellensburg, Washington, in the beautiful Kittitas Valley. It is here that I was introduced to therapeutic horsemanship and I am now a PATH certified therapeutic riding instructor at Spirit TRC, which is where I have spent my free time for the last eight years. This new trail of writing as I ride and work in therapeutic horsemanship is as exciting as any I have ridden.

I can be reached at suelapp16@yahoo.com

Holy Tears and Rawhide Trails

Sue Lapp

PATH Certified Therapeutic Riding
Instructor at Spirit TRC

"I wear my heart not on my sleeve, rather it slides down my cheeks, tears of gratitude for what has been given to me by the horses and people who have been vessels to help me heal myself."

This One Vessel

Every little girl dreams of a pony for Christmas. Me? I wanted not just a pony; I wanted the covered wagon, boots, hats, pistol, and spurs.

Please, if you are brave, come ride with me on a long and winding trail. My journey begins in East Los Angeles, a freckled skinny five-year-old little girl who is so shy, she barely speaks. I am totally entranced watching the show *Rawhide*, while riding my Palomino rocking horse named Star, in my living room. I am brave, swinging my homemade lasso and shouting, "Head'm up, Move'm Out!" There was something empowering about it even at this young age, that I didn't understand. Our old black-and-

white TV made me a star too. Singing "Rollin',
rollin', rollin'..." my shyness would disappear into the
hills of the western landscape. I would imagine the
trail boss depended on me to help keep those
'doggies rolling' as the tune goes. Star is awesome as
he cuts in and around those ornery cattle, keeping
them in the herd and safe from the predatory wolves,
Indians, or even cattle rustlers. My imagination was
always in high gear when riding my horse. Give me
some Clint Eastwood, my hero, and I was a happy
cowgirl.

   We move from LA to Santa Maria a few short
years later, where life changes as it does when one
goes from the city to the country. I fell in love with
this town. There is a western store on Broadway with
a life size horse on the roof! We meet a family with
a daughter my age and two ponies, not only that –
she knows how to ride and wants company daily. The
ponies are stabled at Suey Park, where there are
about 100 weathered old barns, a bridle path, two
arenas, a trail course and whatever our imaginations
could build to ride around in and jump over! There is
no longer time for a rocking horse or TV on
Saturday mornings. I am riding the real thing.

   Life is idyllic as I look back on it. Isn't it always?
We rode like little Indians, bareback through the

nearby riverbed and adjacent cornfields. I truly became that brave cowgirl – or Indian princess, depending on the day. I was fearless on the back of Mr. Dillon, a wily black Shetland pony, who taught me to stay on bareback as a matter of survival. He had every trick in the pony handbook of getting rid of the rider and getting back to the barn.

Years pass. I rode a retired circus horse, a majestic, black Morgan and about just everything in between. Anyone at Suey Park who had a horse needing exercise and a corral to be cleaned, I was their girl. Finally at twelve, my parents could afford to buy me my very own horse when it became clear to them this was not a phase. I had shown them with determination, hard work and the bruises acquired while becoming a skillful young rider.

When riding my sorrel mare, I have an energy that is both boundless and magical. Nothing is too far away I cannot get there on Sweet Lady, there is no foe – real or imagined I cannot outrun from my perch upon her back. Lady and I are so connected, I guide her using only my legs and a rope around her neck. No bridle, no saddle. The freckles and straight hair, the skinny legs which set me so far apart from my naturally charming, outgoing, curly-haired sister and my beautiful mother do not matter anymore.

Lady's mane gives me a place to cry my daily problems into. She soaks up growing pains quietly and without judgement. "Horses bring the fairy tale to life. A woman on horseback grows in strength, speed and mobility. On a horse a woman is reborn as a mounted Valkyrie who until that magical moment lived only in a dream, she is a savior riding to set spirits free, her own among them." (From *She Flies Without Wings* by Mary D. Midkiff.) This was my childhood.

As a teenager, I discovered a new kind of flying. The change happened almost overnight. At the beginning of my freshman year in high school, I took a hit off a joint often smoked on the way. From then on, I didn't go to high school; I went to school high. Once I started, it became a way of life: smoking pot, experimenting with hallucinogenic drugs and alcohol, all easily obtained. Alcohol and drugs, parties and being a rebel, I was an Indian on the warpath. Now my identity was being wild. Oh, I still loved horses. Often, Suey Park became a place where we could go with a hangover to sleep it off in the hay barn, as much as ride in horse shows on Sunday mornings. Searching. It seems I was always searching and never knowing what I was searching for. What was missing inside? There was an emptiness in my heart I was too young to understand, and I was looking for ways to fill the void. I felt I did not measure up in so many ways. I was not pretty enough, not attractive like my gorgeous, curvy older sister. As a teenage girl, this was an enormous stumbling block. All self- induced and indicative of the difficulties my own mind created throughout my life, I was a born perfectionist. The seven-year-old who sobbed uncontrollably over 99 instead of 100 on a spelling test. This continued throughout life – the dramatic reaction to failure which became numbed by alcohol and drugs.

Sue, the native on the warpath, found a trail and runs off to Washington. There I felt free. Free from the constraints of being the daughter of a respected community leader. No one here knew my family – I could wear Daisy Mae cutoff jeans with patches on them, go barefoot downtown without embarrassing anyone. No one was going to call my parents if I were seen hanging out with the wrong crowd. I fell in love with a teenage boy whose hair was almost as long as mine. As mother tells the story, "Sue went up there to Washington, took a survey and married the poorest boy she could find."

We were both young and he was as wild as me. My drinking was out of control, which was easily justified – all our friends drank, partied, and carried on as much as we did. The marriage didn't last, although we tried it everywhere. Washington, California, and Oregon. Finally, it was done. And I was back in California, the marriage a failure. 99 instead of 100 on this first test of adulthood.

Over the next thirty years, there were two more failed marriages, and the damage done to myself and my loved ones can be compared to the proverbial tornado in a trailer park. I am not sure which was worse - the wreckage on the inside, or the wreckage on the outside. It breaks my heart if you could describe what I had left inside as a heart. It had more resemblance to a war memorial with names scrawled on its walls than a heart. My alcoholism had become the obstacle to the ability to have deep, meaningful relationships with anyone. Family members, friends, and men. Everyone in my life suffered in one way or another.

What has endured is my drinking. At age fifty-four, it is no longer cool or fun and finally the black outs are scaring me. Why the blackouts are scaring me now is a mystery. I had been waking up not knowing what I did the night or day before for over thirty years. The alcoholism has completely taken over. I have alienated everyone in my life. I have been told I need help and AA is strongly suggested. I feel like a helpless kitten who is picked up by the nap of the neck as if by divine intervention and dropped at the Moses Lake Alano Club at 7:00 a.m., on a Monday morning where something happens to me.

My thought was, "these people understand my pain." Honestly, I had not realized I was in pain. Early on, in what I now refer to as my "recovery", I came to believe "these people" are vessels from a power greater than all of us. Broken vessels in many ways, and as Hemingway said, "All of us are broken, that is how the light gets in." I did not have any idea what I was in for the long haul. Something happened to me that morning, and the compulsion to drink was gone. I did not suffer relapses, did not have the shakes, nor did I "white knuckle it" like so many of my fellow sufferers. Like taking a shower, the 7:00 a.m. meeting became part of my morning routine. I too became a vessel, sharing stories that gave hope to others. I became one of "these people" and life in recovery became my life.

How long does it take for years of daily drinking for alcohol to truly leave the system? To stop making a lifestyle out of not feeling, of numbing pain and pleasure. How long does it take? I do not know. I only know it changed. I made friends who were brutally honest with me, who sat with me to explain how to change my thinking, to look at my alcoholism as a disease, not as a flaw that had to be conquered. It had not crossed my mind in years that existing as a functional alcoholic was not living. There came a day when I thought to myself – is this all you want to do with your life is function? That particular moment was both an eye opener and a game changer. The tears flowed every time my heart was touched during a meeting. The quote, "I believe that tears are holy because they show us that the ice of our heart is melting," a quote by Barbara De Angelis, became one of my mantras. I added for myself – it must have been Antarctica around mine. It is not normal for alcoholics to stay sober. It is normal for us to drink. As far as I'm concerned, normal is a cycle on a washing machine.

One evening, I stumbled upon a documentary on the life of Temple Grandin. Temple is an autistic woman whose mother refused to follow the advice of the doctors to institutionalize her as child. I was taken by her story as I saw how she used animals to learn to communicate. Temple did not speak until she was three-and-a-half. She communicated through screaming, peeping, and humming. She overcame all odds and earned a PhD in animal science at Colorado State University. Not only was I impressed by what she had accomplished, I was and still am completely fascinated by her life experience. I was thirsty for more on the concept of horses in therapy. Not really knowing what it meant, I went to the internet to learn more on the subject and discovered there was a therapeutic riding center only an hour away from me.

I emailed requesting more information and received an immediate response sharing there was a volunteer workshop coming up that very weekend and a cordial invitation was issued for me to attend. I was on a pink cloud dreaming of working with horses again. The timing came at a point in my sobriety that was pivotal. I was emotionally stable enough to take on a new personal challenge. I believe there are no coincidences. This was exactly where I needed to be going, physically and mentally.

The therapeutic riding center is nestled in the badger pocket area outside of Ellensburg, surrounded by the hayfields that support the local economy.

Walking into this place, my heart swelled with a sense of peace. I felt as if I had come home. It was immaculate. There was an outdoor arena, pens, a viewing room attached to the tack room, and an indoor arena. The simple touches of boots, western prints and books dotted the space which had many functions. On this day, there are both prospective and returning volunteers. Listening to the director as she spoke about her riders, her eyes lit up and her face glowed as she described how it worked – the volunteers side walk, a horse leader and the instructor. I was touched beyond description as I could see she wore her heart not on her sleeve, it slid down her cheeks. Tears of gratitude for the privilege of working with these magnificent animals and children of special needs. There was a PATH (Professional Association of Therapeutic Horsemanship) video showing children with ear to ear smiles. Children who could not walk were riding, learning to guide their mounts. Gaining confidence. Finding their identity. I remember how I felt as a young girl, with my own insecurities, and how riding gave me courage and strength. It struck me how alike children are with all their many differences. These differences may be special needs, as in physical disabilities, or the anxiety of a shy, skinny freckled face youngster.

I did not hesitate for an instant in signing up as a
Saturday volunteer. I truly had no idea what I was
signing up for, any more than I had any idea what I
was getting involved in when I walked into the
Alano Club two short years before that. I was
following my heart, the same heart which rode Star
on Saturday mornings, watching *Rawhide*. The heart
that is finally free from the numbing effects of
alcohol. Still, I was hoping to work more with the
horses than anything else. I longed to ride again, it
was a physical ache. The rest, working with special
needs, was not what I was looking for. Do any of us
really know what we are looking for? It is now my
belief we are led to fulfillment if we will let it unfold
and not try to control the outcome. The patience
which had eluded me all my life would soon become
a part of every Saturday.

The first Saturday I side walked for a lesson,
everything changed for me. The young boy, who was
autistic and nonverbal, had a crooked half smile that
melted my heart. He was able to understand, and I
could feel it, even though he was not verbally
expressing it. Somehow, I could feel it in my heart
and see it in his eyes. And Lad, the Norwegian Fjord
therapy horse, was steady as a rock. During that first
hour, something happened to me – much like what

happened to me that first hour in AA. I do not need
to understand it. The communication without words
is on a level with the knowing look in the eyes of my
fellow alcoholics during a meeting. The spiritual
connection we cannot understand yet we can feel it.
I was overcome with emotions that spilled over, and
still I was only on the tip of the iceberg.

This was the beginning of my journey towards
accepting and learning who I truly was and that I
may have an honorable purpose in this world.
Becoming an integral part of these sessions and
observing no matter the size or shape of the rider's
body, a rider who is connected with their horse is a
spiritual illustration of the threads which sew us
together as living beings. If the horse could accept
and make compensation for the riders' physical
differences – then surely, I could learn to accept and
embrace my own. This living in the present moment
as horses live – and being a vessel from a power
greater than myself for individuals whose
communication skills and sensory perception were
vastly different than mine.

I am no longer searching for what makes me feel
whole. I found it there. There is a country song that
has become my theme. "I'm begging for forgiveness,
I want to make a difference, even in the smallest way.

I'm only one person, but I can feel it working. I believe in better days. That's why I pray..." This is the duo Big and Rich singing *That's Why I Pray*. I sing this song from the bottom of heart as loudly as I can, and the tears come. Looking back on the selfish and superficial lifestyle of the "work hard, play hard" spoiled individual I was, I am amazed at the simple moments that touch my heart. Forgiveness from the people I hurt. The difference I can make today by showing up and giving of my time and myself. Love and compassion become a part of my life as never before and I "can feel it working". It may be a small way, but it is good and is sacred for me. That barn and arena became my church.

One day a nonverbal angry little boy, suffering from his inability to communicate, entered the tack room and struck his mother's arm – hard. We did what is called a "ground lesson". There is no riding, only time spent in the arena with the horse, the instructor, and volunteers. I watched as Trapper went to this child and put his head in the young boy's chest. The opportunity came for me to do an emotional in-depth piece on myself with our director as a gestalt (focuses on insight in individuals to help isolate the unfinished business that is causing pain) coach and Captain, a golden palomino like

Star, as my equine partner. In that round pen, I
shared my truth, released my feelings, and left them
there in the sand. The baring of my soul once spoken
aloud became my reality, my truth. It is my belief
what is shared goes from the arena to God's ears.
Captain leeches - a huge yawn - which is a release of
the energy he had taken from me – energy now
scattered into the wind. All of us carry the answers
to what we search for inside ourselves. Horses have
the uncanny ability to help us in the healing process.
Our equine partners are honorable vessels, much the
same as we are – contributing to the well-being of
other souls. There are as many lost and hurting souls
as there are starfish stranded after a storm leaves at
low tide. As the story goes, there is a little girl who
throws them back into the ocean one by one. She is
told there are too many to save. Why bother. She
cannot make a difference. Her answer, with a smile,
as she throws one more back in – "No, but I made a
difference for that one." That is how I feel when
there is a breakthrough in communication with a
rider – I made a difference that day for that one.
And it matters. I know in my heart I have no
control, as the instructor in the middle of the arena,
over what takes place with a child on the back of a
thousand plus pounds of horseflesh. I can do
everything possible to prevent an accident and

practice safety. At the end of the day, I am merely a vessel for the feelings which transpire between horse and rider.

I ride again, as a part of becoming a certified instructor. The first day it comes back to me and I'm sitting on the horse with a skill I thought I had lost forever. I feel the joy in every bone and vein of my being. I am that brave, daring cowgirl once more. I received the message of hope that comes with recovery and the reaching deep inside yourself to what truly matters in this life. It brought me back to what I loved most and so much more. Not the physical trappings of success, the being a part of something so much greater than oneself. A vessel of basic human decency and compassion. The minutes of split-second gratitude, that turn into days with a fullness of heart, I put into teacups of joy so I can hold on to and reach for them during those dark times we all have. There is an inner nourishment here which is sunshine to my heart and food for my soul.

Learning from horses, whose whispers come from the heart, and children who are not verbal, that behavior is a form of communication. It is about living in the moment and savoring precious breakthroughs. Communication of any kind can be a cry of pain and frustration or an attempt to share love. Understanding time is a non-renewable resource to be used wisely and with compassion for all other beings.

The trail ride, that began on the back of a rocking horse in East Los Angeles, has led me to a therapeutic riding center in Eastern Washington. It has been painful and beautiful. It continues to be both as I learn to mute the negative voices, and listen to the positive, silent messages that come from a divine force I do not need to understand. Where I learn there is no one size fits all solution, we are all having a unique experience. Where I am part of the miracles, which involve work and are a recipe of love, faith and hope sprinkled with dashes of honor, integrity, and the approval of dependable sources.

God made the horse from the breath of the wind, the beauty of the earth and the soul of an angel. My ride in this life has been blessed to share it with this living vessel of the goodness in our world, both physical and spiritual.

"That is the real spiritual awakening, when something emerges from within you that is deeper than who you thought you were. So, the person is still there, but one could almost say that something more powerful shines through the person."

–Eckhart Tolle

Amy lives in Norwood, Pennsylvania. She is a seasoned professional in health and healing, bringing deep-seated knowledge of the human anatomy and heartfelt compassion and care to everything she does.

As a Registered Nurse, her extensive 20 year experience stretches from cardiac care to gerontology and drug and alcohol recovery. In 2011 she added License Massage therapy to her resume, working within spa environments and developing her own personal clients.

Since 2014, she's branched into energy healing, studying various modalities like Reiki, Integrated Energy Therapy, Matrix Energetics and Theta Healing to become an accomplished practitioner.

Amy utilizes her innovative intuition with each client to assess their negative core beliefs and patterns to transform them. She unifies all her gifts as a devoted wife and mother while dedicating time to the crafts of teaching, nursing, massage therapy and energy balancing.

In her spare time Amy enjoys reading, writing, meditating and spending time with her many children, grandchildren and great grandchildren.

Contact: Amykatherine12@gmail.com

Website: www.Handsinsymmetry.abmp.com

Amy Parris

Registered Nurse, Licensed Massage Therapist,
Energy Healer

"You will teach them to fly,
but they will not fly your flight.
You will teach them to dream,
but they will not dream your dream.
You will teach them to live,
but they will not live your life.
Nevertheless, in every flight,
in every life, in every dream,
the print of the way
you taught them will remain."

— Mother Teresa

Two Spirited

"I hate you!" he said, tears streaming down his face, red with anger. My heart pierced with pain as though shot by the arrow of his words. No parent ever wants to hear those words from their child. My child is furious at me, for words I have not uttered, feelings I cannot voice and general confusion of how to lead at this moment. A swell of disappointment arises within me. I say to myself, "I am sorry I didn't understand you. I can't go back and redo my reaction to your declaration. I am sorry I did not believe you were declaring something which would impact the rest of your life." As a nurse, massage therapist, energy healer and empath, I have helped countless other people see past their pain and move into healing. At this moment, I don't know how to help you, my own flesh and blood.

I deeply questioned myself and my integrity. Did I abandon you? When I was a child, I was put in the position of caring for my siblings after Mom left. As the oldest, I felt it was up to me to keep things together at home, watching the kids and preparing meals, so my dad could work. Drama, abuse, and trauma surrounded our family life. It was an easy decision to leave after I graduated high school at the tender age of 17. I desperately craved a normal life.

God had other plans. When I met the man I am married to now, I already had a son. He had custody of his two biracial step grandchildren and so together we made a family of five. After we were married, our family grew. We ended up having three more, making us a family of eight! I remember my cousin messaged me and said, "Eight is enough!" I laughed. We were one, big, diverse, and boisterous family! I was no stranger to assumptions and challenges surrounding our children. With so many varied backgrounds, our kids were bound to hit icebergs now and then. However, my world was about to change in a way I could never prepare for, when my first baby girl was born. I was used to boys, so when the doctor said, "It's a girl!" I said, "Are you sure? Maybe you didn't find 'it' yet?" Something inside me knew and I had a hard time choosing a name. It didn't feel like I was carrying a girl. I believe even in the womb, this child was trying to tell me something.

Growing up, I had been a tomboy. All my cousins were boys. I had to be tough. At two-years-old, my child was already exhibiting signs of being a "tomboy", just like me. As she grew, she rough housed with the boys, climbed trees, jumped off bunk beds and mischievously set booby traps for fun. She always kept me on my toes! She was extremely competitive and always tagging along with her older brothers.

At 9-years-old, she came running to me, blood streaming down her legs. I was sitting, reading my book, when I looked up and could see the panic in her eyes.

"What happened?" I asked.

"I fell," she said.

It would be revealed that while she was playing pool side she fell, with one foot on the concrete and one foot into the pool. She landed in a horrible split. My heart stopped. I was triggered into heightened alert due to my own sexual abuse background. I immediately took her to the hospital. I was a momma bear, standing at the hospital room door. It felt like an eternity waiting for a female gynecologist to come. No way could I bear the thought of a man placing his hands on my child down there. That's the year everything changed. I wouldn't find out until later; this had been a catalyst for early puberty.

Empathic abilities come naturally to me. They are a gift in my chosen professions as a nurse and massage therapist/energy therapist. Yet, when it comes to my children, sensing their feelings can be a double-edged sword. I could really feel things were changing for my daughter. She was pulling away from me, transforming in small and big ways. I noticed my daughter was playing less with her female friends. Friends she had since kindergarten. She was teased by these former friends. I was confused and angered by this. Did the parents of these kids approve of what they were doing? A vivid memory for me is the day I watched her beautiful, long locks of hair being cut off. Tears welled up in my eyes, but I couldn't cry. Thinking to myself, "It's only hair, right? Perhaps we'll donate it." Then, slowly, all clothes that were feminine in any way were replaced with her brother's hand-me-downs. I noticed when we went shopping; she only wanted to purchase boy clothes.

Others noticed too. The moms at soccer practice were interested in why my daughter had cut her hair so short. I shrugged and said, "She said she likes it." What could I say? I didn't really understand myself. Their prying eyes made me uncomfortable. I told them we had donated the hair. The words felt empty to me, like I was making excuses for something. I knew something deeper was going on. Blinded by my own denial, I wasn't able to let myself think about it further.

One day I stumbled upon my daughter contemplative and continually texting on the phone. I walked over and caught some of the words.

Unknown girl: "Why did you cut your hair?"

My daughter: "I don't know, I wanted to."

Unknown girl: "Do you consider yourself to be a lesbian, bisexual or a tomboy."

My daughter: "I don't know, a tomboy I guess."

Who is this person talking to my daughter and using these adult words?!! I was angry and worried. They were trying to put a label on my daughter. They were putting ideas in her head. I told my daughter, "I don't want you talking to her." I didn't want to punish my daughter by taking the phone away. I knew I couldn't block people from messaging her on this messenger app. Things were escalating quickly. I didn't like it.

As time went on, the changes kept building. I had brought the children to the movie theater. As I was in line getting popcorn, I heard this loud, rude voice. "Get out of here! You are not supposed to be here!" I looked across the lobby to see a camp counselor yelling at my daughter! My heart stopped. My short haired daughter, dressed in her boyish way, was being helpful and holding the door for the girls heading into the bathroom. The counselor had assumed my child was a boy and reacted angrily. I was so embarrassed for my child, who was now being publicly humiliated. I wanted to go over and give that counselor a piece of my mind! I knew if I caused a scene, it would just embarrass her further. As I made my way over to my daughter to comfort her, she whispered angrily. "Don't ever ask me to do that again!" I gulped; I had asked her to help out. After that day, she never went to a woman's restroom again.

Not too long after, my daughter asked if she could start taking "T". "Testosterone?" I hollered, not fully understanding the implication. Scared of what was actually happening for my twelve-year-old, I didn't and couldn't handle the reality of the moment. I only know I viewed it as a threat. My beloved child seemed to be at risk. As her mother and protector, I felt like things were out of control.

Instantly flashing back to my childhood, feelings of overwhelm arose within me. Back then I had been unable to control what was happening to me and the people I loved. I was far too young and looked to authority figures who were not as present as they should have been. This time I was the parent and could ask for help. When I reached out to talk to our family doctor, he was very dismissive and suggested my child see a psychologist. My daughter had already refused traditional counseling. She agreed to visit with a music therapist but wasn't comfortable enough to speak with her either. The therapist couldn't give me answers. She did suggest I read the book Parrot Fish, by Ellen Wittlinger. She said, "I think your daughter may be going through something similar". As a working mother and wife, I purchased the book, just never found the time to read it.

One day, to my surprise, a whole gang of boys rode up to my house on their bikes. My daughter had made new friends. It was nice to see my daughter happy again. However, when she asked me if she could sleep over at one of the boy's houses, I became upset. I thought to myself, (only the words actually left my mouth) "I don't know what world you are living in, but in my world, girls do not sleep over at boy's houses!" I could see she was uncomfortable.

She replied, "You're corny, Mom." She quickly left the house. My phone dinged. I had a message. As I read the words, my heart stopped. "I am not a girl. I am a boy. My name is Michael[1]. Do you accept me?" I was speechless. What could I say? I quickly gathered my wits about me and instinctively knew the only thing I could say that would protect my child at that moment, was tell my child I accepted him. "Of course I accept you." I said. "It may take me a little while to call you Michael." I had no idea what I was accepting. I just knew my child needed to know I loved him. Inside, however, the guilt and worry were eating me up. What happened to my little girl? Did I miss something? Did someone hurt you? Did social media brainwash you? I was supposed to keep you safe.

Having six kids all needing care and attention, I am sure I missed some clues as to what was going on with Michael. New words entered my vocabulary, Transgender, non-binary, gender fluid. My husband

[1] The names have been respectfully changed to protect the identity of those in the story.

and I immersed ourselves in learning about
transgender children. I finally read the book
recommended by the music therapist. This was at
least some insight on what my child was
experiencing. The book is written from a female to
male transgender teen's point of view. I started
having compassion for what it felt like to be him, the
awkward feeling of being uncomfortable in your own
skin. Feelings of being judged at home and at school.

"The best gift you are ever going to give someone…
The permission to feel safe in their own skin.
To feel worthy, To feel like they are enough."

Seeking help from my local community, I didn't
find a lot of support. Our child was too young for
the few LGBTQ support groups in our area. The
local children's hospital had a program, but there was
a long waiting list to get in. The stars aligned, and we
were lucky enough to attend a trans-wellness
conference. There were many seminars on topics we
hadn't even thought of. We heard testimonies from
other parents. Some of the kids were younger than
ours, most were older. It was stressed to us pronouns
were especially important. Say he instead of she, and
him instead of her. A presenter at the seminar, a
male to female transgender adult, informed us while

transgenderism became widely known in the 1950s, there are depictions dating back some 9000 years ago. Being transgender is not a new thing. The presenter also touched on one of my fears about using the gender affirming bathroom. She said, "When I go into the bathroom, I am in a stall with a closed door. If someone follows me in there, they're getting punched!" I laughed; her words helped to alleviate some of my worries. I started to have hope my child was going to be okay.

The dreaded day came when my husband and I had to speak with the school. We wanted to support our child the best we could, and it required being upfront and honest. Our transgender child was going to have to face many things beyond our imagination. I expressed my concerns. I wanted this transition to go easy for his new school year. It was comforting to know there were other transgender children in the school district. The school seemed to be agreeable to our requests. However, we were told our son could not use the boys' bathroom. The only solution was to use the nurses' bathroom, which was inconveniently located down two flights of stairs and opposite the middle school hallway. I flashed back to the humiliation at the movie theater. Even though I initially viewed this as a reasonable plan, I knew our son would view this as one more way to make him stand out, instead of being accepted as a boy. I knew this would be a battle for another day.

As the meeting was ending, the principal told us at the end of last year, half the kids on the playground had already been calling him by his chosen name. Our child had come out at school before he had even told us. The mother's heart in me was tormented. I felt very conflicted. If anyone should have been able to accept what was happening, it should have been me. I was constantly sad and worried about his welfare. I would think quietly to myself; this isn't the life I wanted for my child.

As a nurse, a pill could be provided to chase away the pain, heal a wound, cure an illness. I couldn't heal the internal struggle my child was going through. However this pain wasn't something within my abilities to fix or heal. My child was struggling and I was worried about many things for his furture. Will he ever have a relationship, fall in love, and get married? Our interracial grandchildren had been judged many times for the color of their skin. How would Michael be perceived?

With all of my mixed emotions swirling, it was heartbreaking to witness my child pull away from me. He believed I did not accept him. "Perhaps he needed to prove his masculinity," I wondered. My fears were justified when he started hanging around with boys who were rough. These boys were bullies who fought often and weren't afraid of stealing things. He started getting into trouble at school. The school counselor had been helpful through the years, but things were changing. Instead of asking for help, my child was now in open rebellion.

I honestly believe he made some of those teachers uncomfortable. Truth be told, he was making me uncomfortable. He was pushing boundaries in me I didn't even realize I had. He knew who he was. He was not apologetic about it; he was defensive!

His acting up came with consequences. He was literally one step away from being expelled, when the school suggested he go to an alternative program. This alternative schooling was for kids who had been temporarily kicked out of the high school. My 7th grader was being put in a small classroom with troublesome high schoolers! I allowed him to go to this alternative program against my better judgement. I never imagined this would lead to what happened next. Arriving home from work one day, I found him with a bunch of new friends smoking weed. I called him into the house to say it was time for these kids to leave. He was already high while I was speaking to him and therefore not listening to a word being said. As I was trying to find out why he thought all of this was okay, he kept texting on his phone. So, I took the phone. His immediate response was to lash out and attack me. He started hitting me, yelling, "I hate you!" Angry tears coursing down his face. "You don't care about me! Give me back my phone!"

At that moment, the grace of God washed over me. I will never forget it. It was like I was in a dream state. Taking hold of my child I wrapped my arms around him in a huge bear hug until he stopped hitting me. I was unbelievably calm and rational. Soon after, I drove us right to the Children's Hospital.

He was still in an agitated state and the hospital, upon examination, suggested Michael was of harm to himself as well as others. His behavior had spiraled out of control. My child hated me and believed all his pain was my fault. I was starting to believe it myself. The "experts" wanted him committed. I could only agree and cried as I signed those papers, feeling as if I had officially failed as a parent.

The statistics say 80% of transgender children, who

are not supported, commit suicide. The thought of losing my child frightened me. The advice we had been given early on, stressed not to let our child see if we were struggling with their transition or we could lose him.

Michael spent a whole month in the hospital and preferred not to see me. The staff informed me he didn't even want to see my face. You can imagine the deep hurt I felt. He was not quite a teen, and transgender put him in the unique position of needing a private room. There was never a room at the psychiatric hospital available, therefore he did not receive the counseling I felt he needed.

I searched within myself to try to heal why I was so resistant to this change. The wounded little girl in me screamed I had let my child become a victim. As a healer, I believed he needed to be healed. Slowly, I started to remember Michael was happiest just being him. My child loved who he was. It was time for me to start loving him too! After a month, the hospital felt Michael was no longer a danger to himself or others. So they discharged him.

While we had encountered many issues with the insurance company, Michael's hospitalization helped us to get the coverage we needed. This was a miracle! My child was now eligible for family-based counseling. This was the answer to what we had been looking for! Finally, the whole family was able to talk about all that had happened. It wasn't taboo anymore to bring up our feelings. The transition our child was going through was also happening to the whole family. Through family-based counseling there was still resistance, but he began to believe we were there to support him. Our child was coming back to us. We created a space of trust in the family again after so much turmoil. The counselors also helped me realize I needed to grieve for the little girl I had "lost", so I could start loving and building a relationship with the son I had.

The school had promised to use our son's chosen name. This was indicated as a nickname on paperwork. It was not his legal name. Days when there was a substitute teacher, they would slip up and call him by his old name. I could feel his torment. Every time someone messed up his pronouns or called him by his 'birth' name it was a blow to everything he was. It degraded his sense of self. Finally, I agreed to change his name legally. When we filed the papers, Michael was grinning ear to ear. I had to hold back tears once again. It had been so long since I had seen that smile. We planned a Name day party to celebrate.

It's no secret to friends and family that Spirit speaks to me in visions during meditation and in my dreams. Frustrated and confused, I had been asking God to help me understand my child. One night I had a dream. I dreamt I was back in grade school. I was playing with my friends. I was dressed like a boy. I didn't really pay attention to my clothes. People expected me to dress this way, so I did. One day I felt more like a girl. I decided to wear a pretty yellow dress to school. When I got to school, my friends looked at me as if I had committed a crime. I started to feel very ugly. I felt their mistrust of me. I was very unsure if they were even my friends anymore. The following day, my friends started making fun of me. All of this happened because I felt pretty and followed my instinct to wear a dress.

My dream made me realize, on a deeper level, Michael's actions were not a decision. It was his desire to be who he authentically was. God was showing me what had been on the inside, was showing on the outside. I am a spiritual healer. I spend a lot of time helping people heal their trauma and patterns. I have found most beliefs people hold are based on things they experienced when they were children. I thought if I could help my child find whatever the incident was that made him decide it wasn't safe to be a girl, I could help him heal it. I was thinking about the cruelty and the hard life my child would now be faced with. For his protection, I wanted him to change his mind. That was my job, to protect my child! I was so very wrong. God showed me. Being a boy was who he was on the inside. My fight is not with my child and who he is. My fight belongs to anyone who wants to harm him because of who he is. Whatever body parts my child was born with does not define who he is. Michael defines who he is.

Until this dream, I had been doing my job as a parent, but my heart had held back. My love had been on hold, held up by a difference in opinion and fear for my child's future. He could feel all of this, and that's why he rebelled. If his own parents couldn't accept him, why did anything else matter? At 12-years-old, it had been him against the world. He went seeking acceptance from peers. What they thought of him became most important. He told me one day, after we had been in counseling for a few months, "I know how to tell the difference between my real friends and my fake friends now, Mom." I want to say I am sorry for so many times I wasn't there for him, I hadn't seen him, only my trauma. I know he was learning a lot. Learning things you can't teach with words. Learning how to be the man he is becoming.

Love was the key. Love unlocks all kinds of doors even when we don't understand where they may lead. Love is a gift which streams to us daily from whatever beautiful source we all were created from. When we are in fear, we are not in the vibration of Love, therefore we are not thriving. My fear almost made me lose my child.

Other traditions, like that of the Native American people, call transgender people, the "two spirited". I trust that. I genuinely believe the children coming out as transgender are here to help heal the feminine and masculine energies on the planet. What better way to dismantle the old patterns and stereotypes than within your own self. It's not a them versus us mentality, and it's not an easy life these kids have chosen. I can definitely see their role as a healing one to teach us how to drop out of limitations and into possibilities.

"Let your life be a reflection
of your resilient spirit...

strong enough to stand up
when needed...

yet fluid enough to go
with the flow."

– unknown

Theresa is a practicing certified Medium, Energy Healer and Trance medium from England, who is passionate about helping others rise from the ashes of their past. She is also a Spiritual teacher but knows we continuously learn from one another and a teacher will only show you where to look and not what to see. Being highly empathic, Theresa's poetry and writing reflect the inner challenges she has faced during her life and the wisdom she has gained from them. As well as writing and poetry, she has a deep connection with music and plays several instruments. She has experienced music as a great healer, as well as a confidant many times.

Theresa is able to communicate with animals both in spirit and living, which she uses in her mediumship, healings and to locate lost pets. This is fueled by her love of all animals as she believes no life is more important than another.

She has seen spirit as far back as she can remember, and her spiritual gifts have helped her stay connected to the divine within her as her source of strength. She understands the human side of us is separate and is capable of making choices that affect others negatively, which has enabled her to love those considered not so lovable. Her inspiration comes from the many amazing people she has met on her journey who have loved, nurtured and helped her to grow spiritually.

thesymphony@hotmail.com

https://www.facebook.com/mediumandhealertheresaneale/

Theresa Neale

Certified Medium, Energy Healer,
and Trance Medium

"I wear my scars with pride
to show others
they too can heal …
all warriors have scars."

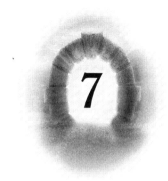

The Symphony

Did you ever have imaginary friends? I did! I used to talk and play with them and sometimes set a place at the table for them.

Did you ever think, perhaps, they weren't imaginary?

You see, they lived in my head. The stark reality unfolded over several years, the insiders who lived in my head did not stay in my head like I thought.

There was confusion and horror of becoming aware of each other, and it caused so much distress and pain for us all. Imagine as a young child, trying to make sense of many voices, and no one believing them. The dark, unforgiving world grew bleaker each day. We attacked each other as if the fight were between us. Our ability to rationalise, that once upon a time we must have all been one, disappeared with every shred of security we had previously known.

I share the symphony with you, to bring you into my world, instrument by instrument, tone by tone, to create a melody one can comprehend and appreciate.

♫ *A symphony has many parts that come together as one voice, we are the symphony, and this is our song. It's a song of pain, our heart pain, and we sing together as one, we are nothing alone – we are the symphony* ♫

I always said, 'People live in my head'. Such a crude and immature way to describe others who have different names, ages, and characteristics. I was a child when I first said that, and it has always stayed with me, but they are so much more.

They live in an internal world inside me, with long winding dark tunnels which go on into eternity. A place where the voices on the outside become more and more distant the deeper and further you go. There is a bright, airy room right at the centre where you can hear everything in the outside world. You are safe from prying eyes and do not have to perform on the stage we call life. These places are safe, but the pinnacle of security is the place we call the dream. The dream is the dream beyond reality, a place of unknowingness and ultimate safety. I know because I have been there many times! Do you have an inner world?

The entrance to the dream is in the central room. It glows with a calming blue light that swirls and pulsates, beckoning you to step inside. As you step through, a peace enfolds every fibre of your being and lifts you, as you float along a river of joy, past trees of the brightest greens, browns, and golds. Majestic mountains reaching into the clouds whisper their great knowledge and power. I believe if you were to climb them, you would surely reach the gates of heaven.

This is the girl that can fly, I heard them say. In this moment, I was being mocked by an older group of girls at the school, while others were laughing at me. It was a horrific feeling. I wanted to crawl further inside and run away. How did they know? Who told them? This would be my first of many confusing moments in my life. I was not prepared for any of them.

From a young age, I would often tell people I could fly, and my story was brushed aside, regarded as an endearing fairy tale of childhood fantasy. I knew the truth, I could fly, but soon stopped saying it to avoid the ridicule which ensued, when I refused to put childhood fantasy aside as I grew older.

I can fly beyond myself
fly beyond what seems to be
be still, listen, dream
the dream becomes reality
I can fly beyond the night
fly beyond my greatest fear
be still, listen, dream
now I can fly, I'm not here
In the dark I hear a voice
echoes of a symphony
be still, listen, dream
I am the dream the dream is me

It was disgusting, I just wanted to wipe the wet, cold film from my face! It stung its defiance, as the chill in the air hit hard, claiming its victory, with the threat of being repeated if I wiped it away! Is it okay for a man to kiss a three-year-old this way? It had to be since he was a relative, didn't it? This wasn't a normal kiss, and I disliked it intensely. Something inside of this little girl felt it was wrong. The older I got, he touched me in ways that were uncomfortable. He told me it was a secret. I was so sore when he touched me in places I had never been touched before. It hurt and I didn't like it. Be quiet, he would say while I just wanted to fly away. My eyes gazed upon his parrot and wished I could have those wings to get away from here, from him. I would be pulled deep down into a dream, a place beyond reality into a bliss of unknowingness. It was a place I felt safer and away from people like him.

I understand, now, this was a process called switching. However, the ones who live inside knew this and a lot more from the very start. The term switch means to change. For me, this change was when one of the people in my head, the insiders, swapped places with me and lived my life. The voices in my head would get louder, ready to stand in my place, each time a situation, a trauma, or something uncomfortable would face me in life.

Why does there always have to be one of us who has to front? Who will do it? Who is going to take the burden of excruciating pain or unfathomable rage? The fastest? The strongest? The smartest? The bravest? Who, who, who? We can't let her stay there, she will die if she stays and fronts, but it's too late! One of us is thrust into the outside world ......
SWITCH

There would be many painful years upon us all, yet we would each explore every inch of a wondrous place. The dream is a world inside us that is separate from reality; it became our reality and reality became the dream. Its vastness, filled with glorious and vibrant colours, was the refuge we sought during the storms which invaded our safety. The sun was warmer, the water crystal clear and everything in this new reality became magnificently alive. A world that swallowed us away from the cruel, unforgiving darkness in the outside world. The birds became a part of us. Their songs had a melody we wished we knew, not the same as the song of the symphony. It was here we learned to fly.

A long way in the distance on the other side of the dream is a door that stands strong and erect. Only those bold enough can walk through. It is a door which leads to limitless possibilities and a shadowland of the outside world. You may understand it as a gateway or portal, but we see a door calling us to experience the wonders beyond it. As you take that brave step and walk through the door, the safety of a veil covers you, and holds you within a blanket of peace. The veil hides you, as you fly to places, meeting people you want to see, where the iniquity and corruption of man's inhumanity can be observed from a safe distance. The veil covers and holds you safe, so you don't have to be a part of the world's selfish acts or desires done in secret. You can observe them for your authentic self, as if you are right there in those private spaces, with those who believe their evil deeds are unseen.

In this place, you can also watch other ways people live, the fun and joy they give each other, or visit other worlds not like ours if you choose! Hidden from view, behind the veil, you can manipulate everything as the unmovable loses its power in this place. The door to this world is the entranceway that transcends time and space. Many others, besides us, have found the door to this world in their own way. There are few who have visited it often or have learnt the secrets, because the fear of being seen stops many in their tracks, and they dare not explore any further.

Have you ever seen the film *Sybil?* It was based on a book and is the story of a woman who was diagnosed with multiple personality disorder. It is now known as dissociative identity disorder.

As I continue to take you deeper into the melodic life of the symphony, allow me to explain us better to you. We are many, and the world has provided a name for us, so others can understand us better, perhaps? It is with great courage and excitement we reveal to you how we came to know and understand, somewhat, the medical terminology which has been provided to explain what we experience.

In *DSM-5* (*American Psychiatric Association, 2013*), dissociative identity disorder (DID) is described as a disruption of identity, characterized by two or more distinct personality states or an experience of possession. The clinician may observe or the patient may report that these personality states demonstrate marked discontinuity in a sense of self and/or agency, accompanied by changes in effect, behaviour, consciousness, memory, perception, cognition, and/or sensory-motor functioning. In addition, the person experiences dissociative amnesia, a disruption in autobiographical that includes gaps or difficulties in recall of everyday events, important personal information, and/or traumatic events.

I have always loved God and all the insiders too. I read my bible every day growing up, and at thirteen, I went from place to place searching for answers. One of these places had a closed-minded belief system, and it wasn't long before they noticed the insiders. They said they were demons, and I believed them! They tried to cast them out of me with many exorcisms, and my soul became tortured with each failed attempt. Why wouldn't they go? Am I not trying hard enough?

Thousands of questions spiraled in my mind, and fueled by fear, they grew out of control. My thirst for answers could not be quenched, and the confusion suffocated me.

I spent many hours alone, as the guilt, shame, and rage grew until my inner fear began to destroy me. The torment of my soul spilled into my poetry, music, and thoughts. Why didn't God save me from this nightmare I was living? 'Why didn't he save us?' I am Evil! We are evil!

There was a battle within me, the nightmares were relentless and were of unimaginable evil. My mind was filled with visions of shadows that came alive when I slept. I prayed constantly for God to take the shadows away, and I fought to stop them from consuming me. I had flashbacks of things I couldn't remember and overwhelming panic attacks. I was drowning, but I kept it all inside of me. I lived between these two worlds, the normality of daytime and the evil which stalked me when I was asleep.

When I came back from the dream, it would be so confusing and often frightening finding that hours had passed. Had I really been in the dream for that long? Everything around me was so different. Nobody seemed to have noticed I had been gone at all. One of the insiders had lived my life again!

Who are they? What am I? I am a monster, we each uttered repeatedly until we believed it with every fibre of our being. We would all find out many years later God had so much more in store for us than this.

My innocence led me to people that would continue to bring harm and abuse to us. Shocked, terrified, and ashamed, it took years to realise what abuse was doing to us. I finally began to put the shattered pieces of our lives together and realised the abuse from my relative at a young age was unacceptable. After he died, I let the secret out. I told my mum how I was touched and kissed by him. I did the one thing I was never supposed to do. Tell the secret!

My mum told me he had left me a substantial amount of money in his will. I sobbed and sobbed. All the presents he had bought me, all the money he had given me, and now he had left and named me in his will. Was this payment for all I had done for him? Why had God let this happen to me since I was a child? I heard the insiders saying, 'Why had God let this happen to us, we are a child too.'

There are far too many abusive stories to tell you and they would cause you nightmares if I shared each one, or about the countless vile people, who perpetrated these acts. These events are hidden inside my mind by those who dwell there, safe from the cruel world outside.

Here is a small glimpse of some of the pain we express through our poetry.

The wind outside made a terrible moan
But I'm here safe, all alone
Only the light from my room
Shone out bravely in the sultry gloom
Outside stands a ghostly form
without a face and clothes all torn
But I'm here safe from the evil outside
I'm here safe, I've somewhere to hide
Voices are talking inside my head
They speak of a world beyond the dead
Is this the reason I was born
To be haunted by this evil form
I'm so afraid, why don't you hear
Does anybody out there even care
The voices drones on, a monotonous tone
Help me Lord I'm so alone

After I left school my life began to change, and the horrors of my childhood soon faded. I grew into adulthood and began to forget there were shadows lurking in the back of my mind. Life was good. Still things happened that reminded me all was not right in my world.

I had stored away all the pain and trauma and ignored it. I wanted to be normal, and I was achieving it. Then my world completely fell apart. My mum got ill and was soon given her prognosis there was not much time. I loved my mum with all my heart and soul, she was my caregiver, my confidant, my best friend, my world. I was so young at the time, newly married and with a young baby. How on earth would I cope without her? She has gone, what do I have left now??? There is nothing left at all! Inside my head I could hear them saying the same, 'How will we cope without her, she is our mum too, she has gone!'

After Mum had passed, the grief began to consume us all, and all the pain we had held inside for so long, began to spill over and envelop us until our soul was crushed. The symphony all had a story, we all had a song of the atrocities we each had endured. As the horrors and darkest pain fell from each one's mouth, our descent into madness sped faster and faster. Some carved their pain in red lines on our body, creating a makeshift map of an untold story within us in an attempt to allow the pain to spill out. Some burnt their misery into our flesh to brand us forever with words unspoken and the quiet ones kept their pain inside and took pills when they thought we weren't looking!!! Our scars and mutilated body did nothing to relieve us from our misery, our soul was weeping with tears of regret that all we are meant for was to be hurt and destroyed. This isn't life, we want to die!!!!

As we took each pill
the relief grew and grew
soon it will be over
and this life too,
this hell this shame
and the secrets inside
would soon die with us
And forever hide
Pill after pill
Just a few more
keep going don't stop
We fell to the floor

I was hospitalised and with each treatment I heard the insiders less and less, their presence in my life grew weaker but when they didn't go completely more treatments followed. They weren't voices to be silenced, they were people who eventually learnt to be quiet and stay in their inside world.

Shh... can you hear us?
We are crying in here
We're crying inside so you can't see
All the pain falling from our eyes.
Can you hear us?
We are fighting to believe
Our story isn't over
Our story was far from over!!!

We left the hospital with medication, which came with life destroying side effects. I was a shell of who I should have been, and from within the prison they held me in I started to dream of a life different from the one that had been prescribed to us by those who didn't understand.

We continued to take tablets in an attempt to destroy who we were, and all that we had become. The tablets we took had turned into our hope to be free from this pain, a lifeline to gain back what we had all lost. Eventually our body could take no more and we had a near death experience and as we were about to go into the light, I saw my mum!! She gave me the choice to go with her or to come back for my children. I had seen my mum!! She hadn't died at all. Her soul lived on into eternity and so will ours. I had seen her she is alive; how can my gifts be evil or wrong? I had seen my mum and my gifts were a gift from God to be cherished and nurtured.

Slowly at first, I embraced the gifts I had always had of mediumship and healing. I was a natural; I knew that because I had always seen and heard spirit since I was very young. I quickly saw that all I had been.

Every day I felt more compelled to follow the path that God had laid before me. I didn't need courage to do that, I had already shown courage during my life with what we all we had endured. What I needed now was to accept us all for who we are and love us in the way that God loves us.

Why can't anyone let us be who we are? I am not crazy; I was abused!!!! The decision was made as quickly and simply as that; we stopped all medication. I had battled the ghosts of my past all night long; and now it was morning. The symphony started to sing to each other and within each ballad held the hopes and dreams in the sound of the loss of a life expected. We heard each song and held them with arms of love. We had a very long way to go, but we were starting to heal.

You can draw? That's amazing!!! And what about you? Poetry? Music? Wow, me too!!!

We sung our pain, we sung our joys, and sometimes yes, we sung about toys!!!

Laughter soon became a piece that would sing in our hearts. Our gifts began to develop more as we understood each other and worked together to support each one. Everyone is so talented and gifted, and now we incorporate it into our spiritual work. I had no idea these gifts would bring me to a place in life where we can help others.

Our mediumship became more profound with so many of us involved as well as healing. Didn't God say, "Where two or three are gathered there I shall be also?" It dawned on us all, one by one, we are perfect just as we are. Although many don't understand how there can be so many people in one body, we don't understand how there can only be one. It is as different as the moon is to the stars, but they both fill the night sky, and all have their place and are needed.

I continued with my mediumship. We learnt many

things together. One thing we learnt was when we do trance mediumship, we do it differently than others who are just one. If we feel safe enough, we can all make a decision together into the dream where the outside world doesn't exist, and allow spirit to use our body. We are in early development but we are truly humbled for all the years that the dream was our refuge to escape the pain we were enduring on the outside. God has now turned this around to be a blessing to us in our trance development and many other things.

When things happen to you, that cause you to become different from others, don't think for one minute you aren't meant to be here. There is always a light at the end of the tunnel. Everyone is right where they are meant to be, nobody is higher or lower than another person. Everyone is different, but we are all equal and needed just as we are in the universe. Don't copy the person you most admire or want to be like, the world already has one of those. The world needs one of you, just as you are, regardless of who you are. I am grateful for what we went through because now we have the tools in our toolkit to help others and nobody's pain is more or less than another's. Going through any trauma is a blessing, because it is training!! Training to use the divine tools and gifts that have been freely given to us. God does not put us through more than we can handle, although it seems like it at times. We grow through what we go through to learn a skill that is needed in this world to create balance, harmony, and love.

We are growing more and more each day, and now know spirit didn't leave us all those times we thought they had. They were preparing a way for our future; the future and life we had all planned together before we came to this physical world.

We are the Symphony and we are still singing to each other and one day we may sing more of our song to you and who each of us are. We were never the monster in our story, those that caused us to be this way by what they did to us are the real monsters.

We aren't broken, we are the symphony, a shining multifaceted diamond with fourteen sides!

"Go inwards,
find your inner space
and suddenly you will find
an explosion of light,
of beauty, of ecstasy."
– Osho

By the time we reach adulthood, most of us have had to overcome and recover from something. Siobhan's story includes not just persevering through, but overcoming and actively recovering from childhood trauma, mental health issues, substance abuse, homelessness, cancer and most recently, tearing her knee during competition. Siobhan states her purpose in life is "to inspire others into action." Using both her personal experience and the knowledge she has gained through education and a career in research and treatment, she works to offer hope and inspiration to anyone who feels stuck inside the circumstances of their life.

Currently, Siobhan works in the mental health and substance-use disorder industry. A primary focus of her role is to develop and evaluate programs addressing the opioid crisis and to share the findings with the industry at large. She regularly presents original research worldwide, has published multiple articles in peer-reviewed scientific journals, and conducts education within the addiction services network. She is a voluntary adjunct faculty and serves on policy and advocacy groups in Washington DC.

In her spare time, she is a CrossFit Masters athlete. She has consistently ranked top 5% in her age group. The recent knee injury has not dampened her dreams of competing on a world stage. She lives in Columbia, Tennessee.

Samorse10@aol.com

Siobhan A Morse

MHSA, CRC, CAI, MAC

"Fall seven times
and stand up eight."
~ *Japanese proverb*

Go Ahead
and Kill Me

Go ahead and kill me.

I'm naked, on the athletic field, standing next to one of those portable buildings on the campus of an elementary school somewhere around midnight. There is a man in front of me waving a machete and speaking to me in Spanish. I reach for the cigarettes in his front shirt pocket and say, "Go ahead and kill me." In that moment, I never-ever-ever would have believed that my life could turn out so different.

It was a Friday night. Maybe Saturday. I just know Calle Ocho, the colorful, famous street in Miami at the heart of Little Havana, was alive with the smells, sounds and sights of a busy party. There were a lot of cars, most of them playing music loudly. A mix of hip-hip, big band salsa and electronic dance music filled the air. Near the intersection I was approaching, the smell of garlic and Caribbean herbs was heavy. People gathered at the window of a restaurant buying Cuban pastries and small cups of espresso with loads of sugar called cafecitos.

I was feeling pretty cute walking down the street, sashaying my hips, almost dancing really. I had made my outfit myself and felt pretty sexy, even though in my mid-30's. I was by far the oldest girl out walking tonight. There was a gentle horn tap which caught my attention as I approached the corner, just on the east side of a large parking lot for a strip mall. When I looked over my left shoulder at the street, the driver nodded his head and began to pull into the parking lot. I approached the car with my sexiest smile, cutting my eyes across the parking lot and adjacent street to look for police cars.

The car was a few years old, a two door, neatly kept, as the driver appeared to be. He was late 20's and seemed uncomfortable speaking to me. His brown eyes held embarrassment and looked away as he asked me if I was working. He appeared to be Hispanic, normal for this area of Miami. His accent was weird, or maybe he didn't hear well. The sounds of his words were imprecise. He pulled the passenger door handle and pushed the door open for me.

I slipped into the light brown interior of the car and sat on the cracked faux leather seat. As soon as I had the door shut, I turned slightly toward the driver who was still not looking at me and tell him we should get a room. I let an implied threat of police hang in the air, as I told him it would be safer in a motel room, directing him just two blocks away to The Cabana motel.

I was flush with victory, as he pulled into the square-shaped, dead-end, cracked asphalt parking lot, surrounded by a u-shape of rooms, the office directly behind us on the left of the entrance, almost closing the "u" into a square. The door creaked as he opened it, pulling the keys with him, and walked to the safety bar covered window which provided access to the "office" and "manager". I might have nodded off to sleep for a moment, sitting in the hot car. Sweat beaded on my upper lip and I could feel a trickle sliding down my side from my armpit. It was humid, and I didn't want to be smelly already this early in my night. A shower would be nice.

When he returned to the car, he slid into the seat, offered me a key attached to a hand-cut piece of laminated white cardboard, on which someone had written the number 6 with a black wide tip marker. His calloused outstretched hand also had $40 in it, which I greedily took and turned to get out of the car. I could feel the roughness of his hands, slightly clammy palms, as he grabbed my left wrist to stop me from getting out of the car. Not hard, but firmly, implying we were definitely doing this his way. He told me, in slightly broken English, he wanted to go to his house. He'd gotten me a room, and said it was for me later and insisted we go to his house. He still had not made eye contact with me. It was a strange moment for him to be looking slightly down and to his right, into the foot well of the car at my feet. I considered the key and the money, shrugged, leaned back, mumbling "Whatever." And we headed back out of the parking lot.

The car was quiet inside, except for the rumble of the older engine and the sounds of traffic and music coming from outside. After pulling back into the traffic on Calle Ocho, we quickly turned right. We were only a block away from a residential area. Two blocks later, we turned right again, doubling back a couple blocks behind the shopping mall. Although I had been round and round these streets endlessly, it was always at night and always felt like a labyrinth to me.

We drove for less than five minutes, although I can't be sure. I shot up the last of my heroin shortly before setting out on Calle Ocho that evening. I was in that space where if I wasn't moving I was prone to slip into a light sleep. The movement and warm breeze coming from the car's window might have lulled me into another nod. Time really had no meaning to me at that point, but I knew it was more dangerous to fall asleep. Besides the obvious, he might steal back the key and the money.

As a working girl, there is always danger. Each minute you spend with a customer, you are taking a calculated risk. The movies would have you believe there are "rules", like never get in a car with more than one male, never go to someone's home, always make sure someone sees you get in the car. That's all bullshit. The only rule is do the deed, get the money. End of story. No one is out here saving up for college. We all need something, and cash transactions are the way life is measured out here.

I measured everything in how much heroin it could buy. Heroin is the warm embrace, complete with the murmur of sweet, shushing sounds you've always needed so badly. It's like God Himself is hugging you, which is good because outside of heroin, I'm pretty sure God hates me. There's this beautiful moment, just after you push the plunger, where you just know that no matter what is going on, it's going to be okay. And you can finally exhale. You're not ecstatic or anything like that…you're just finally okay, at peace, back in the womb. I would do anything for that feeling. Anything.

The movement stopped. I was awake as we pulled onto the grass, on the outside of a low fence enclosing a sports field for an elementary school. He was pulling the handle on his door and pocketing the keys in a single motion, as he mumbled to his closed window his house was on the other side of the school. I just assumed he had done this before, probably with some of my friends, and this was how he avoided nosey neighbors. Maybe he lived in the little apartment on the back side of one of the small brightly painted houses, as so many of my customers did. He said something else in Spanish. Although I can generally understand, he had moved to the back of the car and his accent was still strangely unidentifiable. I could not understand him.

I had stepped toward the open lid of the trunk, around the rear passenger side of the car. We were maybe two feet apart; his back to me briefly and reaching into the trunk. He quickly turned toward me just as I reached him, and I saw it. I had no time to react. The rough hand returned to my wrist, grabbing it forcefully this time, and he finally looked up at me. I saw his brown eyes for the first time. They were filled with anger, meanness, maybe hatred or disgust. He no longer remained the quiet, embarrassed young man who had picked me up. He seemed stronger, bigger, almost looming, despite being barely taller than I. He was holding a machete in his other hand.

I was gone. Not physically. Emotionally, I checked out, vanishing deep inside, like a hermit crab. I can only imagine how vacant my eyes looked, even more than my usual drug-induced far-away stare. I joined the tens of other me's, where we hid from the pain of being screamed at, beaten and raped. The me who had gotten in that car, was gone for good.

He still had hold of my wrist, closed the trunk with his elbow, and was pulling me toward an opening in the fence. I was looking down, trying to think, a million thoughts flooding my head. Yet I could understand none of them. I was stumbling a little as he dragged me across the uneven ground, and I rolled my ankle on a clump of grass, dropped slightly, enough for him to feel the pull down, but I did not fall. He yanked my arm harder. I trudged across the wet crabgrass, and through muddy spots where the puddles had been after the afternoon storms, typical in Miami. I was sweating from the exertion, from the heat and humidity of the Miami night, and from fear. I could hardly walk across the seemingly ginormous field in the big, clunky heels that were a size too large, and I stumbled a few more times. He just kept pulling me, staring ahead through the yellow street lamp lit night, at a cluster of small buildings that looked like tiny, one room houses on a prairie. As we get closer to the buildings, I know I'm moving toward something awful. Something really terrible is going to happen and I'm resigned to it. I just don't matter enough for anything or anyone to save.

The glow of the streetlights and the buildings appeared to be yellow. Both of us were in the shadows now. He stopped me by pushing me down between two of those buildings. We were invisible to anyone who might casually pass through the field.

The tip of the machete felt cold and sharp as it pierced the skin at the hollow spot on the base of my throat. He pushed hard enough to make it bleed, just a little. He told me to take off my clothes. I took off the outfit I had felt so sexy in less than an hour earlier, and plopped down on the concrete step in front of the building's door. He took my shoes too. Threw everything out of reach, out of sight on the side of the building. He just stood there, pointing the machete at me, while I sat on the stoop.

I'm terrified he is going to use the machete to have sex with me. I reach for the cigarettes in his front shirt pocket and say, "Go ahead and kill me."

Anything would be better than being penetrated by the machete. I feel like I've spent my entire life waiting to die. What's strange is, I'm not even afraid of dying here, not the way I should be. I'm sad, just eternally sad.

He responded to my request to just kill me by re-puncturing my throat with the tip of the machete. He forced me to face the wall, with my legs spread and my hands on the wall. I could hear him opening his belt. I did not cry. My unwillingness to beg, despite the fact I would not cry, was ruining it for him. I gritted my teeth, stifled the gasps and went to a place deep inside. It kept getting worse - I was getting pounded, torn and ripped apart. Something inside my head told me to whimper. It was me, but not me. I just wanted to find my way deep enough inside where it didn't hurt, so I ignored the voice. She insisted, telling me it was the only way to make it stop. So, I made a pathetic sound, then another and pretended to cry. Not thinking about what would happen afterward, I was listening to that voice. She was getting me through this. He finally finished with a grunt.

As he held the machete to my throat one last time, he told me if I moved from this spot before he drove away, he would find me again and kill me. He set across the field back to his car. Spontaneously, I began to use the blood from my throat to write the words, "I was raped here" and the date on the wall of the building. I still didn't cry. I can still see the awkwardly written letters, almost as though a child wrote them. I think it was the child in me that was hiding but wanted to be heard. She wanted her voice back, the one she had learned to surrender to survive. She needed people to know what had happened, again. She wanted to believe how we turned out wasn't her fault.

I'm dirty and bloody now. A drizzle of blood has dripped to the collar of the shirt I'm wearing. I have dirt and blood smeared on my face and my clothes. I'm so disappointed and sad about life. It's as though this was another example of how unworthy I am and how much, whatever God there might be, hates me. I am certain I will never know anything good because there is something so deeply and so completely wrong with me. I was lost, figuratively and factually, trying to find my way back to where this all began.

Let's face it. We all sell out sometimes. Sometimes we sell our values or our beliefs. I sold my body too. Not just for the money. I needed to be wanted. It was how I experienced my sense of self. I had learned early on how I looked, especially my body, was what determined my worth. It doesn't matter who or how at this point. If you were sexually abused and raped as a young teen, taken advantage of as a young woman, or if the only way you knew how to feel like you weren't invisible, was to perform sexually, you are not alone. This was just the evolution of needing to be seen or heard, to be approved of, to earn your favor.

It's ironic my superpower was to dissociate, to disappear when I wanted so badly to be seen, to be heard, to feel loved. From early childhood, I learned to go away, deep inside, where no one could hurt me. I created images and people in my mind and in the person I presented to the world to protect me. Perhaps if I'd spoken up, told someone, expressed how I felt and what was happening, things could have gone differently. That's not as easy as it sounds. As a child, we have almost no voice. Adults need to speak for us, to protect us, to be our voices.

Eventually, on a night like the one on Calle Ocho, where you can hear the palm fronds rustle in the warm breeze, the puddles still fresh on the asphalt, I reluctantly and unwillingly sat through a therapy group. In hindsight, I can see the seeds being sown. "Of the 16 people in this room, only one of you will be successful after a year", and I heard the protective voice in my head, the "other me" say, "I hope you guys are all okay." Same voice which pulled me through the Calle Ocho nightmare, flipping off the world and letting people know I was going to make it. Letting me know we were going to live to see this abundant harvest of life I still had left in me.

I had no idea the harvest would be this life I have today. No longer homeless and addicted, I have published articles on treating substance use disorder in scientific journals, appeared as an expert on radio, television and at conferences around the world – all with the hope my research and experience can help others transform their lives and the lives of their patients. I am an executive in a Fortune 500 health care company and a competitive master's athlete. I have also had the opportunity to mend relationships that matter to me, like the one with my parents. I love and forgive them and myself for what we did to each other. Although they have passed, they are with me, loving me and proudly encouraging me so often now.

Amazingly, I found my way back to God; despite having lived in fear of Him and sure of His disdain for me most of my life. At the time of the Calle Ocho events, I was certain if there was a God, He was mean, unforgiving and must certainly hate me. Yet I now know the only reason I was able to survive that night and am alive today, is because something or someone had been helping me all along. I feel as though I was being watched over and protected the entire time. I know now I can rely on this always

Initially, I was unprepared and fully unwilling to consider the existence of the God of my childhood: the white guy with the beard, the blue judge's robe, sitting on the throne, on a cloud holding that gold stick and judging me. That guy, he hated me. Once I began to consider the possibility the image I had of God was not God, it allowed me to begin to dismiss the idea that I know what God looks like. Perhaps if I let go of the image, the feelings I have about God will also change. I could not even use the term God. I said Higher Power, Divine Intelligence, Source, Universe, Creator and other terms. Anything to remove the negative emotional charge from the concept.

As cerebral as all this was, it was sinking in at other levels. I was learning intellectually and emotionally. I realized one day, I did not need to beg forgiveness from that old man in the sky. If He really is God, He knows everything I did, everything that was done to me, and I never shocked or surprised him. So, I thought, maybe the only one who has to forgive me is me. If the Creator of everything doesn't need to forgive me, who am I to need to forgive myself?

I heard the actual words I was saying to myself, probably for years. All the ways I told myself I was not good enough. The feelings had always been there, but I'd never heard the words clearly. These feelings always seemed like the truth to me. Affirmations became a part of my daily routine. To me, they were things that weren't true yet. Gratitude lists helped me shape the future of my life. Sitting in my tiny single room of an apartment, I would smile and work to generate a feeling of gratitude, then write lists of things I both had and wanted in my life. Practicing self-generating gratitude taught me I could generate other emotions and live life from a positive perspective.

I experienced the wonder of everything around me and could not help but consider the kindness, the love with which everything was created, and the intelligence that had to be behind the symphony of all life. This brought me closer to the Creator. My trust in Divine Intelligence who created our wonder-filled world kept expanding. It was as though I was waking up for the first time. I was waking up in His arms, no longer hiding from the world, safe in His embrace.

I realized this Divine Energy is not just "out there", but it is "in here" too. That same thing which created everything there is, the Source of all this beauty and mystery around me, is in me too. Something shifted deep inside me. I began using the term, "the greatness that is in me," when I considered or spoke about God or the Universe. Often, when I would consider this greatness, I would nearly cry. It was overwhelming, in all interpretations of the phrase: How wonderful I was so divinely protected! How intimidating there IS greatness in me! How terrifying I could live big enough to fully express this greatness in me!

The negative patter in my head was often the words and feelings of a child. I called to her and all my little girl selves, at all the ages where we had experienced things that were terrible enough to make us run and hide deep within. In a secret place in my mind, with a beautiful cabin in a clearing covered in lush tropical landscaping next to a pond with a waterfall, we met each other. I held myself as an infant, held the hand of a three-year-old version of myself, and hugged my eight-year-old appearance. I apologized for leaving them and told them I loved them. Over time, so many came of different ages. I do not have the memories which sent them into hiding, and I did not ask for them. I simply loved them the best I knew how. Although I did not know it, I was learning to love myself.

I'm wearing my new outfit tonight. I feel pretty, as I walk toward the elevator, in a posh high-rise in the exclusive Downtown Brickell neighborhood in Miami. My hips sashay and I'm almost dancing really. A bell dings tastefully and I enter the elevator. The dark, brown wood is contrasted with mirrors on the walls, brass hand holds and expensive marble tile.

As I'm keying the code for the private floor, I catch a glimpse of someone in the corner of my eye. I turn to look at her. As I look into the mirror, I see a woman whose eyes are clear. A hint of a smile graces her face, her head held high. She is strong, beautiful, powerful. She is an overcomer. I am proud of that woman. She is the woman that as a little girl, she'd hoped to become. A Wonder Woman. No longer on heroin, I get to be the heroine of my own life.

Conclusion

You're thinking... day in and day out "What if?"

"What if I took a chance to do something different? To make a change in the way I act, dress, think? What if I tried something totally new for me, without any fear, and just decided to go for it?"

But instead you think, "NAH, I'm good here, hiding behind these sunglasses. I can peek out and watch the world and be an observer. I'm doing okay, so why do I need to change anything? I am comfortable here."

You dream though. You dream of a different life and sometimes you feel guilty about it. You may think "It's not so bad. I have a nice place to live and a good job. Am I just bored? Am I being selfish desiring something more for myself?"

Yet, there is this yearning and calling inside to explore, to have adventure and freedom , to see the world, to learn about other cultures. Maybe you want to paint, to dance, to learn an instrument. Perhaps write a poem or a book. You feel something inside pushing you.

"Nah, it's crazy, right? How could I possibly do that? I have no time. I don't have enough money and it just doesn't make sense." Did you just make a bunch of excuses?

There are lots of voices that create doubt. These are the old beliefs that limit you. These are the voices that control you and make decisions to keep you in your comfort zone. These are also the voices you can learn to empower, to release and to quiet down.

I know life is short! What if you took an opportunity just for the fun of it? That's easier said than done though, right? What if something went wrong? What if you came home and you had no job? What if you decided to stay in this new place? What if ... what if?

What if you woke up feeling ALIVE!? What if you met people that saw you for who you really are, without any judgments? What if you got to experience things that were once only a dream and it shifted your perception of living? What if you met like minded people who understood you? What if a whole new world opened up to you that brought you so much joy and opportunity? What would you do?

The journey has always been about honoring and loving yourself fully. You are here to accept your gifts and receive this love from source without denying your talents and greatness.

You were born to love and embrace the process of growth. You are here to remember your spirit and blossom in this human form. You are here to live the way it was intended by your soul's purpose and never according to someone else's beliefs, rules or judgments.

The more you love yourself, the more light will shine upon the world... this universe.

Every person deserves and has the right to see their beauty and glory. Everyone deserves love, because we are born from love.

The true essence of our journey is to transform the world. We were not sent here to be complacent. There was never limitations on you. Keep expanding your heart at every sunrise... take the opportunity to glow, to be bold, to rise up!

In a humble space of wisdom our spirit appears in our thoughts, words and actions. It inspires you to move to greatness, not from a place of ego, but from a place of the omnipresence of our source and all that is.

We were conceived from the greatest love ! You said YES to be here! Re-member your spirit's purpose, for you were placed here to gift the world with your message.

In loving thoughts I hold your purpose in the highest love, from the source of all creation and so that you live a life of love, always and forever.

Gloria Coppola
excerpts from *You, Were Born to Love*

"The most important relationship is the one you have with yourself. Learn how to develop self-love and connect with your true essence."

Channeled Message

RELEASE OLD PARADIGMS:

We are being asked and guided to release the old paradigms that we have been living by for centuries. Old, outdated paradigms around working HARD to succeed, working at things we hate in order to have a "good life." The new paradigm is about creating joy in who we are and what we do, and trusting that we will be even more abundant in every area of our life by doing so. Follow our passions, embrace ease, actively pursue JOY, for these are the currency of the new world.

RELEASE FEAR:

We are STRONGLY being guided to release FEAR! Fear of the unknown and fear of LACK has kept humanity enslaved and trapped for centuries. In this current time of upheaval and change, the fear of not enough (money, food, supplies, jobs, safety, health) is constricting so many and keeping them from standing up and reaching for the light that is waiting for us all. Release all old fears and the ancient paradigms around MONEY. Trust and know that there IS enough for everyone. Believe that all is well and take steps in accordance with your highest and most good. Your are loved and protected in all ways and all things.

PUT DOWN THE ELECTRONICS!!!!

While phones, computers, and television are your current means of communication, the over dependence on electronics has become a detriment to your world and your race. The addiction to electronic media of all types is not only an addiction as severe as drugs or alcohol, it is also an avenue for fear and negative energy to gain traction in your minds and your own energy fields, allowing dark thoughts and dark energies to seep in and take control of your minds. Monitor how much time you devote to your electronic gods. Do not give them control of your mind and soul. Step away from the temptations they bring and instead shift your eyes and your heart to the world around you, that you can touch and see and feel. Give your love and your energy to those around you. Connect through your heart and your hands. Keep your lights alive and burning brightly to see the coming of the age that we are bringing through you. Awaken from the slumber of the ages and behold the world we are creating before your very eyes. Awake, rejoice, create and be joyful in the new world that is being wrought.

All of creation speaks, if we only are quiet enough to listen.

Accept and embrace where you are at RIGHT NOW, who you are, what you are doing. There is NO going back. What you were in the past is gone, never to be again. Stop hanging on and wishing for that which is gone forever. Even if you are able to reclaim something from the past, it will never be exactly the same as it was, for all things change. Change is the constant in the Universe. Even tomorrow, you will be different than you are today. Let it go. Release the desire to be what you are no longer and look forward from this moment, from this point, and create what you desire from here. Nothing will ever be what it was again. And that is a good thing. Embrace it, accept it.

Stay in your Heart. This has never been more important than it is right now!

Channeled on July 21, 2020 for all of Humanity

Intuitive artist and designer, Candy Lyn Thomen, who did the layout for this book and our other Powerful Potential and Purpose Publishing books, is also a channel. As the year 2020 began to unfold, the world slowed to a near halt, and life as we knew it began to drastically change, the messages she was receiving also began to change. The over-arching theme of these new messages was self care, self love, rediscovering who we are at the deepest soul level and honoring that in our lives. For the first time, Candy has shared the strongest, most prevalent message she received.

Don't Go Back to Sleep
Rumi

Today, like every other day, we wake up empty
and frightened. Don't open the door to the study
and begin reading. Take down a musical
instrument.
Let the beauty we love be what we do.
There are hundreds of ways to kneel and kiss the
ground.

The breeze at dawn has secrets to tell you.
Don't go back to sleep.
You must ask for what you really want.

Don't go back to sleep.
People are going back and forth across the doorsill
where the two worlds touch.
The door is round and open.
Don't go back to sleep.

I would love to kiss you.
The price of kissing is your life.

Now my loving is running toward my life shouting,
What a bargain, let's buy it.

Daylight, full of small dancing particles
and the one great turning, our souls
are dancing with you, without feet, they dance.
Can you see them when I whisper in your ear?

All day and night, music,
A quiet, bright
Reedsong. If it
Fades, we fade.

Spiritual Awakening
Journal

What are you noticing is out of balance in your life?

_____

_____

_____

_____

_____

_____

_____

_____

_____

_____

_____

_____

_____

What can you do to align yourself?

Are you having synchronous events in life? List
them below so you become more aware of the
messages from your soul.

When do they seem to happen?

_____

_____

_____

_____

_____

_____

_____

_____

_____

_____

_____

_____

_____

Do you find yourself feeling emotional? What
events may be triggering the onset of emotions?

Are your dreams more lucid?

Write down the things you remember daily. You may notice a pattern or a message.

_____

_____

_____

_____

_____

_____

_____

_____

_____

_____

_____

_____

_____

Does your health seem to be affected by life events?

_____

_____

_____

_____

_____

_____

_____

_____

_____

_____

_____

_____

_____

_____

_____

What can you do to stay healthier and stronger?

Take time to meditate this week. Journal below any
insights you are having.

Are you avoiding signs? Why? Fear, doubt, confusion? Stop for a moment. Ask your soul what you can do to trust.

Take 5 seconds and respond below.

_____

_____

_____

_____

_____

_____

_____

_____

_____

_____

_____

_____

What inspires you, brings you joy?
What is your passion? Is there one thing, or several,
that light the fire within your heart?

_____

_____

_____

_____

_____

_____

_____

_____

_____

_____

_____

_____

_____

_____

If you could do ANYTHING in life, what is the next step you need to take?

_____

_____

_____

_____

_____

_____

_____

_____

_____

_____

_____

_____

_____

What do you feel or think your soul purpose is in life? If your inner voice says, "I don't know," then imagine what it could be and write it below.

_____

_____

_____

_____

_____

_____

_____

_____

_____

_____

_____

_____

_____

_____

Do you sense a breakthrough is coming?
What does it feel like?

Are you ready for a breakthrough? Listen to the wisdom of your soul for guidance.

Write what you feel below.

_____

_____

_____

_____

_____

_____

_____

_____

_____

_____

_____

_____

_____

Once your breakthrough happens, what is on the other side?

Write about what your soul guidance is telling you.

www.PPP-Publishing.com

Gloria@gloriacoppola.com

828-713-3521

Made in the USA
Columbia, SC
22 October 2020